ReWrite Your Story

by Cledra Gross

Cover Photo by Calvin Evans, www.CalvinEvansPhotoshoot.com

ISBN-13: 978-1502707611
ISBN-10: 1502707616

Acknowledgements

To my Mother, thank you for being a mother, friend, and sister through it all. You have called me almost daily and I know I wasn't always the most grateful for those calls in the moment, but know that I am most grateful for them now. Many days you helped me reframe the darkness. I continue to feel your prayers and your love, even when we're not in the same physical location. For this reason I know that independent of our physical time left we will always be together. I thank God for the gift of having a woman as phenomenal as you to call Mother.

To my Father, thank you for always pushing me to dream big. You challenged me to do the best in anything I decided to do. Not many women can say they had a dad who was always there at every field day event, every birthday party, every piano recital, and every parent-teacher conference. Every time I said, "I need ___," you filled in the blank with what I was asking. God blessed me beyond measure when he decided to choose a man like you for me to call Daddy.

To my baby, thank you for flooding my body with more love than I've ever known by allowing me to see you and hear your heart beat for the time allowed. I'm grateful your spirit continues to guide me and encourage me as it did the day I found out you were gone to be with God. "Go back, Mommy. Go back," you said. Well, that's what I did. At the time, I didn't know what I was going back to, but with your help and our Creator's hand, I have come to realize why it was your time to go and not mine. Night, night, my baby. I'll see you in the morning.

To the reader of this book, I say thank you for taking the step to drop all of the unnecessary weight preventing you from living your best life. Your best life starts right now and I'm grateful for your permission to allow me to support you through the words in this book. There are 8 chapters in this book and you can read them in any order. The intent is that you have a handbook on standby from this day forward that can help you when you feel the weight of life being added. I also want you to know that I hope this book isn't the only way we interact, but more the beginning of a friendship that will last for as long as it's mutually beneficial. Please visit me at my website www.planbecoach.com and on Facebook at www.facebook.com/planbecoach. I would love to hear from you and to continue to support your efforts to drop all unnecessary weight through the inevitable challenges of life.

As you read this book, my wish is that every word goes into your heart, and as a result your heart will beat with lighter weight. Who would I be had I not lost it all? I would still be asleep to my best life. Becoming awake to your best life is my single intention as you turn each page.

The events in this book are based on my best memory. Names and some locations have been changed to protect the identity of the wonderful people who have intersected my journey and assisted in the many life lessons I present. I don't claim to have the perfect memory with the perfect timeline, but I do claim to have an intention to serve and elevate the skill set of every person investing their life minutes to read these words.

Table of Contents

Chapter 1:

The Weight of Contradiction and Conflict

I'll stay until you become who I think you are in my mind…

In some ways graduate school felt like I had won the lottery. I had my own apartment, enough money to not have to work two jobs, and the flexibility of a schedule that didn't include classes every day of the week. This was going to be my time to live my life the way I had always imagined.

Against my parent's advice, I got an apartment on the basement level. God bless them, they knew the statistics of women who were assaulted in every state and how my apartment location increased my odds. I love my parents dearly, but sometimes their hyper-vigilance caused me to want to intentionally be on the edge. There was something about being vigilant that made me crave throwing caution to the wind. I got my white furniture, bright pink fake flowers, and the dollar store artwork together in no time in my new apartment. I was finally in a place that I could have my say in how things were going to go.

Gold's Gym was right down the street and my first step was to get color-coordinated work-out gear to make my debut. The gym always had nice eye candy and I was visualizing how things were going to be different once I got my weight in order.

As I was leaving my apartment, the door directly across the hall opened and there he was – chiseled like an ice sculpture made from frozen honey.

"Hello neighbor. My name is Honey. And you are?"

I wanted to say, "Dayahm, I am whoever you want me to be" but my conservative Southern Belle upbringing managed to make its way out of my mouth, and instead I said, "Hey, I'm Cledra." All I could think was how happy I was to have my cute outfit on because this man was definitely going to the gym. Hell, he looked like he lived there. We had that eye contact where you know this is going beyond an introduction. The chemistry was immediately in the air, my hormones swirling like a bee examining Honey's every feature – his lips, his chest; his... well... his everything. And I could tell he felt the same.

All of this went down in five seconds, and then Honey said maybe we should go out some time, and before he could finish saying "some time", I was, like, "Sure, how about tonight?"

And the rest is history. Honey had been the runner up in the Mr. North Carolina pageant and was working to get his pro card in body-building. Meeting him was like adding more credit hours to my graduate work in the topic of losing weight and building a fit body. Boiled eggs by the dozen, tuna at every meal, steamed vegetables, and steel cut oats all made up my new diet with Honey. His body was his business and, slowly but surely, his body was becoming my business, too.

Honey invited me to train with him at Gold's and it opened up an entirely new world. That's when I learned the difference between working out and training. Honey said that an amateur works out, but a professional trains, and that I had a pro's body, so moving forward I would never work out again. I would train.

Honey flowed into every part of my life. He wanted to pay my rent, take me shopping, take me to Carowinds. You name what a woman could want and Honey was right there to provide, but I just couldn't let him take care of me. I prided myself on being an independent woman and I couldn't help but wonder what kinds of strings were attached to all that caretaking.

My 24th birthday was coming up and Honey was getting frustrated with me turning down all of his offers, so he said, "At least let me take you to Hawaii for your birthday." Hawaii? WOW, that was tempting. I had never been there and the sound of going was wonderful. With the statistics of women never returning from dates looming in my head from my parents' daily bad news updates on the phone, I couldn't help but share Honey's offer with my mom.

"Mama, Honey wants to take me to Hawaii for my birthday for a week!"

"That's great, Cledra."

WHAT? That's great? I was bracing for the statistics about how many women are on the bottom of the ocean off of the Big Island, but Mama surprised me. I said what any woman full of statistics about the death of women her age would say: "Well, what do you think about that?"

She said, "I think it's great, but will you do me one favor. Let's run his driver's license through your uncle." My uncle was a private investigator and I could tell Mama was coming through the back door this time with the CSI spin on me going to Hawaii. But because she was trying to not be as extreme as usual, I felt I could concede, and so I said okay.

While Honey was in the bathroom, I got his driver's license number and texted it to my mother. I didn't think anything of it because Honey and I had spent almost every day together for the last six months. I lived across the hall from the man. If he was a serial killer I think I'd know by now, or worse, be dead. Mama called in a few hours and I could tell from her heavy voice, something was wrong.

"Is he there?"

I said, "Yes."

"Well get rid of him and call me back NOW!"

I immediately dismissed this as one of Mama's classic overreactions. Honey probably had a speeding ticket or a bad credit report, but I respect my mother, so I did what she said and told Honey that I had to turn in early because of an exam. As always, he was very respectful and kissed me good night and went to his apartment.

"Okay Mama, so what did the report say?"

She paused and said, "Cledra, he's wanted in all 50 states for drug trafficking and for murder. You need to get out of there as soon as possible. You are dealing with one of the king drug lords in the South. He has been MIA for several months. The authorities want you to help set him up."

HOW could this be? How could I tell her I was in love with Honey? The thought of setting him up was out of the question. I just didn't believe this kind, gentle man was a murderer. Mama went on to say that I should not have any more contact with him and she made me promise that I would get out. I told her okay, but nothing in me intended to follow her directions. I just didn't believe it. I called Honey over and told him everything. As if the night wasn't bizarre enough, my conversation with Honey took it to a whole different level of cuckoo. He said, "Cledra, what you just did saved your life."

I had just saved my life? I didn't know what Honey was about to say, but one lesson I had learned the hard way was that the voice within always carried more validity and support for my highest self than any voice outside of me, even my mother's. This was especially true in relationships, because when you share what's happening, you share half of what is probably less than half right.

"Cledra, the truth is that I have had you followed the entire time we've been together and that's why I know that your word means something. You've always told me the truth and I know that from having you followed."

"Followed? Honey what are you saying?"

"I'm saying that the information your mom told you is somewhat true. I didn't personally kill anyone and that's all you need to know. I feel guilty meeting someone like you and having the past that I have, because for the first time, you have shown me that something different is possible. I never imagined I'd fall in love with a nerd and love every minute of it. You treat me like a smart guy with big goals. No one has ever done that before. Most people treat me like what they think they know about my past. Until I met you I never felt like I could be anything other than what I do."

Honey never came right out and said he was a drug dealer, but what was clear is that what we had was real love untouched by his alleged crimes or past indiscretions, including potentially murder.

"I just can't thank you enough for telling me the truth. It would've really hurt me to send someone to kill you."

That sentence snapped me outta Fantasy Island, and I realized I was sitting in the presence of danger. How could so much danger and so much possibility to be someone new exist in the same moment?

"Promise me you will come see me in prison."

What? I'm a graduate student with a scholarship. That didn't gel well with prison visits. But in spite of my inner voice screaming to get the hell out of this, I heard my outer voice say, "Yes, I'll come to see you in prison."

What in the hell was I thinking? Oh I know! It was the part about him sending someone to kill me!

A few days later Honey turned himself in. His mother called to thank me because she hadn't been able to keep in touch with him and now she would know he was safe. Honey was splashed all over the news and the paper as my heart was splashed and broken. Not only was I not going to Hawaii, I had fallen for a man who was now going to prison.

I got my first letter from Honey less than a week later.

Cledra I love you more than I ever thought possible and I have something for you when you come to see me. You would never let me take care of you, but you took care of me by being honest and I want to give you a gift.

A gift? What kind of gift could he possibly give me in prison? They were stripped of everything, including their dignity, at check-in, but my word and keeping my word were everything to me. I had been raised to believe that a person was equivalent to their word and people who didn't keep their word or changed their mind were weak and useless. That was the message that, in spite of the conflict with the voice that I had grown to trust, caused me to fuel up, lie to my mother about what I was doing for the day, and take the four-hour drive to prison.

Besides, I was curious about my gift.

The sky was a beautiful Carolina blue the entire way to prison. However, all the energy I got from driving on a sunny day seemed to vanish as I approached the turn. I could see from a distance several men from every angle standing almost like statues, with rifles that had scopes. Even from a distance, they all had a look of "shoot to kill" anyone even thinking about getting out of any door other than the front door. There was at least four feet of barbed wire above the triple layered wire fence.

There was something incredibly sad about the reality of Honey being somewhere between the rifles and the barbed wire, dressed like a hundred other men being told when to do everything other than take a dump. I wanted to make a U-turn, but I didn't know if that could also mean my death. It was no different than the point of no return they talk about in driver's ed; that point where you're going so fast into an intersection that stopping would cause more damage than going forward, even though you're going forward on a red light. All you can do is hope that others will temporarily yield for your insane moment to pass through the crossroad.

I had to remove everything, including my favorite pen, to pass through the series of security checkpoints. By the time I sat down to see Honey, I felt in some ways I was in prison, and the truth is, I was: A prison of being torn about what to do – a prison of lies. It didn't feel good to lie to my mother, but I knew she wouldn't approve of me going there. I mean, hell, I didn't approve, but there I was in prison, literally and figuratively.

Honey and I were in some ways no different. We had both turned ourselves in to face the consequences of a series of poor choices.

Physically, I was in a prison, sitting on a cold metal chair waiting for Honey, while emotionally I was swimming in an ocean of uncertainty. As he turned the corner, my mind and body came back together and I remembered what I felt for him. His infectious smile, the way he made me feel so beautiful, and there was no doubt the man had a body that I'm sure was making every man in that prison take notice. He was fine and he was headed my way. I couldn't imagine what my gift would be.

We were instructed to give each other what I consider a church hug, barely touching each other, which was torture. We sat beside each other just staring in both lust and disbelief that after everything, we were actually sitting in prison having a conversation. It was déjà vu of the moment we had when we met outside of my apartment and we knew instantly there was a spark.

As we sat looking at each other in silence, there was so much we were saying between those same eyes that had fallen for each other. We were in the intersection, the crossroads, and it was going to be impossible for us to pass through and stay in the same vehicle of love. In those five minutes of silence, we ended our relationship.

But what about the gift? Honey finally broke the silence and asked about my workouts and my eating. I told him I had fallen off my program since everything had happened and I hadn't been eating right. He started going into body-builder mode, telling me about how to balance my carbs and to not have anything other than lean meat and spinach for dinner. He was starting to annoy me. Spinach, carbs, working out? Seriously? I was in prison not really understanding why, but I was clear it wasn't to learn how to eat like a body-builder.

Our 20-minute visit went quickly and Honey hugged me to the point where security had to intervene. The last thing he said was, "Cledra I love you, and make sure you eat your spinach." Clearly he was medicated or something because he wasn't making any sense.

As they ushered him out I cried as I passed through each layer of wired fencing and moved past all the long rifles with scopes that seemed to be pointing directly at the top of my head. Finally back in my car, my cell phone was ringing. It was my mother. She was good at detecting a lie in my voice, but I knew if I didn't answer she'd be worried.

"Hello, Mother."

"So Cledra, how long was the drive to visit Honey in prison?"

I was busted. It made me feel like I did as a child when she would tell me that she knew me before I knew me and that I would never be able to fool her. She was right. I paused and told her four hours and that I was about to get back on the road to head back home. Most of the time it annoyed me for my mother to bust me, but in that moment I was happy she had come to visit me in prison.

Later that night Honey's words kept echoing in my mind: "Eat your spinach… Stick to lean meat at night and eat your spinach". He was right. Ordering pizza and eating my emotions away wasn't helping, so I decided to take his advice. I went to the freezer and pulled out a big bag of spinach that Honey had bought, but it looked like it had been opened. I didn't know why he would open the bag and then try to make it look like it had never happened.

I got some scissors to cut the bag because he had taped it shut. As I took the scissors to the top of the bag, I cut and cut and looked in disbelief. The bag of spinach was full of one hundred dollar bills! My hands started shaking. There must have been thousands and thousands of dollars.

That was my gift. Honey had wanted me to eat right so that I would find the money. He couldn't blatantly tell me in letters or on the phone because our calls were recorded and our letters were read. He had carefully orchestrated a way to take care of me without me even knowing or without my permission. It was all coming together. He knew I hadn't been eating right because I hadn't found the money. That's what he meant when he said make sure I have lean protein with my spinach. Very few people, especially black people, ate that way, and so he also knew that I'd more than likely be eating alone if I was having a typical body-building meal.

Just as I finished counting the money the phone rang. The caller id had the federal prison, but I couldn't answer. Part of me felt like this money had blood on it and another part of me felt like it supported the reason I went to prison… Love. This was the most Honey would ever be able to do for me for the rest of both of our lives. Should I let him or should I give it back? But then, how would I do that? I didn't want to think about the answers to any of these questions, so

I just didn't answer his call. I had to walk away at some point and I decided, standing there holding my bag of spinach, that I would start right then.

Sometimes we have to walk away from the people we love because they are not well enough to go with us into the next chapter of our life. And trying to explain that to them would be more hurtful than just walking away. That was my life lesson with Honey. We both knew it was over and yet it was never spoken. We were living a contradiction and it would only cause additional conflict if we refused to drop the weight of "contradiction and conflict".

PlanBE Action Steps to Drop the Weight of Contradiction and Conflict

IDENTIFY:

Identify the areas of your life where you feel torn. Questions to ask yourself are:

- What times do I find myself saying or doing something that doesn't align with my best life?
- Where am I going along to get along?
- What is the price I'm paying for keeping contradiction and conflict in my life?

DROP IT:

Write how life would BE different if you dropped the contradiction and conflict.

Realize that you can stop this tug of war alone. You do not need family, friends, or anyone else to participate in your CHOICE to drop the weight of conflict and contradiction.

REPLACE IT:

Living without this contradiction and conflict would allow me to... Now, write the vision of your life without the weight of contradiction and conflict, but with the freedom of commitment and focus.

Chapter 2

The Weight of

"I Can't Believe This Happened To Me!"

Cledra… You're pregnant! It was the news I had waited to hear for so long. I screamed a scream that brought tears to my eyes. All the visions of my baby, all the vision boards with the positive EPT pregnancy stick, all the nights I cried… God had finally answered my prayers. I was pregnant. OMG!

I called Hershey to tell him the news and, like me, he was amazed. We had been pregnant twice before and lost both of them. I could hear my clock ticking louder and louder and the thought of not being pregnant another year was just more than I could bear. I wanted to be a part of the mommy and me groups, the mocha moms, the kid talk that I had only been able to sit on the sidelines and listen to. I wanted in the mommy game and it looked like I was finally going to be let in. I was tired of the "when are you guys gonna have a baby?" or the "we're praying for you" looks. All the baby blessings, all the baby showers, all the baby talk about daycare… I wanted to be a part of all of that, and I was over the top that my time was finally here.

Hershey took off work and we just stared at each other in disbelief. We weren't even trying to get pregnant. In fact, we were waiting to do blood work to begin IVF.

When God made parents, He really went all out and gave me the best. Mother gave me more love than a child could hold and Daddy gave me more life lessons than one mind could remember. I couldn't wait to share all of what they gave me with my baby. As an only child I used to dream about the day when I'd have a family of my own, kids that looked like me. My secret prayer right after, "God give me a healthy baby" was, "And if you don't mind, can he look like me? And another thing… If you could make him a he, that would be great too." My transition to a woman was a hard one. Being taller than most girls, a little weird in wanting to read all the time, braces that seemed like I had on for a lifetime… The list of things that made my transition to womanhood hard was a long one.

I also imagined family traditions that were just mine. Now it was all going to be possible.

They wanted me to come in the next day for an ultrasound. I was so anxious I could hardly sleep the night before. A baby. No, MY baby! The thought of it was overwhelming. It happened when I wasn't even thinking about it. It all was coming together at a time when I thought it was falling apart. This was the redemption I had been praying for. Surviving Hershey's infidelity early in our marriage. Separating for a year. Renewing our vows to wipe the slate clean. It was all worth it. I was pregnant and life was getting back on track – FINALLY!

Holding hands, we anxiously waited for the nurse to call my name. She told me to get undressed from the waist down and I almost started before she left the room. I wanted to see my miracle. Hershey and I just stared at the blank screen. He was holding my hand as I lay there with a paper blanket over my bottom and my legs in stirrups. Then the door opened and the doctor put what looked like a vibrator wrapped in a condom in my vagina and he said, "Now, if we're lucky, we'll…." thump thump thump "…hear the heart." My body felt like it was being flooded with love, filling up with an emotion so strong that the joy and love I felt made me feel like I might explode. I cried, I smiled, I looked at Hershey in disbelief, and then I couldn't take my eyes off of the screen. There he was… My baby, with a strong, beating heart. It was hands down the most beautiful music I have ever heard. It was like a drummer making music that announced the coming of something miraculous.

"Can you print that picture out?" Visions of a collage from this first day seeing my baby until the day we came home from the hospital were already coming together in my mind. The new doc said that it was safe for us to share the news with others considering how strong his heart was beating. He did say there was a slight chance – about 10% – that something could go wrong at this point, but it was only slight, given everything he saw on the ultrasound.

"Hello Mommy" appeared above my little baby's body and beside it were the words EDD 12/19/07. EDD: Estimated Due Date. "Hello Mommy." WOW… I couldn't feel any better about my life. I couldn't stop thanking God. I had the man of my dreams, living in the home of my dreams, and now looking at the baby of my dreams. God was so good to give me so much.

As the doctor printed my baby's first portrait, he joked about our little miracle and asked if he was going to be an NBA player or play in the NFL? My husband was 6'6" and I am 5'10", so our little peanut was already off the charts for his age. I didn't care if he played the clarinet and twirled a flag. I just wanted him to be healthy, happy, and, between God and me, look just like me. But it was fun wondering how tall he would be. Ninety percent chance. That was really good. I'd take that score any day of the week.

Thump, thump, thump, thump… I wanted the recording of his heart, but they couldn't do that. In my mind I was already thinking of stopping to get a recorder for my next ultrasound. I wanted to soak up every single second of this moment in my life. No one would ever know the depth of pain I experienced aching for my own child. My parents loved and adored me so much I knew that the only way I could survive the loss of their love would be to have my own baby. We had a bond that only death could break and I couldn't imagine bonding with anyone else in any other way besides giving birth.

Because I had miscarried twice before and being 37, I had several other ultrasounds. I looked forward to them like they were a surprise birthday party. I got to see my baby and hear how much he had grown. Nothing in my life had ever made me feel so much joy. Nothing. I finally knew first hand what all of my friends, co-workers, and parents meant when they said there is no love like the love you have for your child.

Mother's Day was coming up and Hershey and I alternated between parents for every holiday, and it was the year to be with his mom. So we headed to DC as usual. But not me. I floated to DC! To me, every day seemed like a day walking on clouds. I could feel my body changing and the fact that it was because of my baby overwhelmed me with gratitude. I thanked God every chance I got for allowing my time to be a mommy. I had never wanted something so much and had to wait so long without being in total control. Getting to DC felt so good because I could finally join the mommy conversation when the women and the men went their separate ways. Before I was pregnant I would join the men because there were times when being invisible was too hard, and that's the way I felt as each woman would go on and on about their children. I didn't have anything to contribute other than a heart that ached to join them. But this time was different. I could finally talk about what it was like to be pregnant. I was finally a visible woman.

The date 12/19 rolled off my tongue like I had won the lottery. I was already thinking about how to make sure HC (that's what we called him --- Hershey and Cledra abbreviated; he was going to be the 3rd anyway, but I wanted to put my stamp on him) would have a great birthday AND a great Christmas. I had heard horror stories from friends through the years who had birthdays in December, and their parents would combine their gifts and they hated it. HC wouldn't have to go through that. Mommy was already thinking about how to make both his birthday and Christmas very special.

I had just one more ultrasound to pass and I was going to be released from the High Risk OB office. After years of working out almost every day, for the first time in my life I didn't care that my weight was well into the 200s. My baby was healthy and I could change my weight later. I floated from DC back to Charlotte as Hershey drove, completely over the top to get the results from my last ultrasound.

"Welcome to your second trimester." I was SO happy to hear that sentence. My first pregnancy didn't go past six weeks, and my second, well, that one is still too difficult to talk about. The third time is a charm, as they say, and no need for me to look back.

Just like before, we anxiously waited for them to call our name and I quickly put on the paper blanket, excited to see my miracle another week later. There wasn't a day that went by that I didn't thank God for answering my prayers.

Silence. Silence… Why couldn't I hear anything? I was looking at the ceiling waiting to hear the thump thump thump thump, but all I heard was silence, until… Until the doctor said, "Cledra, his heart has stopped."

I asked, "Well, what does that mean?"

She looked at me and said, "Cledra… His heart has stopped."

Again, I asked, "Well, what does that mean?"

She grabbed me on both sides of my shoulders and said, "Cledra… His… heart… has… stopped!"

And that time I heard her.

I collapsed. My body and my belief in God collapsed. What about the 90%? You mean I'm in the 10%? Did it hurt when his heart stopped? Was something wrong with him? Did I do too much over the weekend? Could the machine be wrong? Can we get a second opinion? Can you revive him?

A collapse. A complete and total collapse.

Before we could get home, they called to have us to go the hospital for a more advanced evaluation. For a moment, I thought maybe, just maybe, it's not over. We arrived only to find out that the life that might be over was mine. After further evaluation, they said they were very concerned that I might not survive my pregnancy. The location of my baby was in such a place that the recommendation was for a partial hysterectomy. Hysterectomy! It was too much for my mind to process. I had gone from reading a Mommy To Be card the day before, to having to entertain the idea of never being a biological mom.

"No, I will not have a hysterectomy," I replied.

They told me that the other alternative required me to sign a waiver that in the event of my death, neither Hershey nor my family could sue the practice for negligence, and that I was fully educated on the high risk I was taking. Unless you've been shredded to the point of collapse, you don't get that everything they were saying sounded like Charlie Brown's teacher – Wah Wah Wah Wah Wah Wah. The pain is so loud you can't hear anything else other than *I CAN'T BELIEVE THIS IS HAPPENING TO ME*. Shock consumes you; denial comforts you. While I signed the release, it was with a body that no longer had a mind present. I wanted a chance and the only thing I could grasp was that a hysterectomy would destroy my chance. The doctor had told me after my other two pregnancies that once you get pregnant, getting pregnant again is easier. Somehow in all the pain, I remembered that small sliver of hope.

"By signing below you understand that this medicine destroys pregnancy tissue?" I understood what it was going to do to the remains of my baby, but no one could help me understand what it was doing to me. Success on the Doppler ultrasound was if there was less red color and more blue surrounding my baby. It meant that the medicine was eroding his tissue successfully.

It was all very clinical for the doctors. I knew all too well the oath to save lives, and in their minds my life was the only one available to save. But on the inside, my life was crumbling. What I saw every week on those ultrasounds was at times too hard to bear, but I told my therapist my baby could never get too ugly for me to look at him. My husband had told me it was too difficult for him to go to the appointments, so I would go alone. Every week for six months I sat beside women whose pregnancies were advancing, as their bellies were growing and so was the joy in their eyes. I, on the other hand, was there to see each week just how much of my baby's body had been destroyed from the injections.

Being a pharmaceutical rep, I had access to top doctors around the country. I asked one to give me the prognosis and he said he only knew women from the morgue who had pregnancies like mine. He had never seen one survive. In that moment I felt like an outsider walking in a world where I didn't belong. I wasn't a mom, I was carrying a dead baby, my life was at risk, and everywhere I turned it seemed like other women were celebrating their babies. "I'm pregnant, but he's dead" wasn't exactly what people wanted to hear and it was even less what I wanted to say.

So I ate. I ate to appear to be growing, I ate to numb the pain, I ate to medicate myself, I ate to become invisible, because the more I ate, the less people looked at me.

I ate because that seemed to be the only thing that I could do to put myself to sleep quickly. There was nothing like a big country breakfast with lots of syrup followed by a big sugary glass of orange juice to put a woman who was pre-diabetic to sleep for a few hours. Besides it helped me feel better when I'd hear the other women talk about how much weight they had gained. That was my something that I could have in common with them – gaining the weight. It was my first realization that we parent from both sides of the grave.

Similar to those expectant women, I wondered if my baby was okay. Oh, I knew he was dead. I knew medically he was a fetus. But I had seen his heart beat. I had seen him move. I also knew that for me, he was my only child and as his mommy, I still worried. I used to ask him if it hurt for his heart to stop. Yes, once that beating heart makes you a mommy you're always a mommy, in life and in death.

I would wake up to a wet pillow from crying in my sleep. God had spoken. It was over for me. The answer was no. Final verdict. Final answer. God had spoken and that was the end. Amen.

Like every mommy, I needed to know my baby was all right and God gave me that gift. I would repeatedly dream about being on the beach and just over the horizon I could see my baby looking at me as he was being carried. I would run into the water as fast as I could, trying to dive to get to him as he said, "Mommy GO BACK! Mommy GO BACK!" I would stretch my arms to him trying repeatedly to dive to get to him and he would move further and further away, saying, "Mommy... Mommy go back." I would go back to the shore tired from diving and then I would wake up wet.

"Mommy go back." That was my message. But, go back to what? I didn't belong on the shore. I didn't fit in. I was in the 10% and most didn't even want to be around me. I reminded them of the worst thing any woman can be reminded of. I was a nightmare, the wet blanket on the next baby shower excitement, a damper to the conversations about baby weight. No, there was no place for me on the shore. I wasn't sure what my baby wanted me to do when I went back, but I was grateful he stopped by on his way to the other side of the Jordan. Everything in me knew that is what was happening. God had come for my son. Permission to hold him had been denied, but permission to see him and to know he was okay had been granted. It's what every mommy has to know.

HC was okay, but I wasn't. I wouldn't bother being a part of the mommy discussions anymore. I did everyone a favor and took myself to the sidelines to become invisible. I had learned the most difficult lessons of parenting. My baby was in God's hands, not mine. My baby was on God's agenda, not mine, and from the first heartbeat, being a mommy is about letting them go and grow through you. I had that in my head, but my heart was going to need a lot more time to catch up.

"We can take him out." The words I dreaded to hear and the words I needed to hear to save my life came in the same breath. My baby was finally small enough for them to remove without it killing me – at least not physically. All of the needle sticks, the phone calls, the ultrasounds were over, at least for this little one. Six months after his heart stopped beating, they got him out; six long, horrific months of staring at that giant flat screen with EDD 12/19/07 in the corner.

I was already somehow given the grace to dream about getting pregnant again. The doctors had told me that because I had carried this baby for a while and conceived naturally, that the chances of us getting pregnant again were really high. That hope made the six months of living hell worth it. I had a taste of what it would be like to know my baby was on the way. The idea that I could have that again got me up every morning, even though it was difficult.

By this time I had eaten my way up to 246 lbs. I was officially obese and I didn't know it until I went shopping and the size 14s I wore at the start of my pregnancy stopped at my knees. I had lived in sweatpants and elastic waist jersey outfits for the past six months because I traveled a lot for work and that material didn't wrinkle. I dressed in clothing that couldn't wrinkle because, maybe on some level, I felt so wrinkled the thought of having to press something to make it through anything else was too much – even an iron. I thought surely the 16s would work, so I headed to Lane Bryant, since now I was officially limited to the big girl store. But to my surprise, the 16, the 18, the 20, and the 22 were too tight. I had to get a size 24. I wanted to fit in and look like my pregnancy was advancing, and at the same time I was numb with my insecurities of not being pregnant at my age, so much so that I buried myself under extra weight. Reluctantly, I got all the dressy pants they had in my new size 24 and headed home. But not before stopping at the big soft pretzel shop for the BOGO sale. I could buy one sugar coated cinnamon soft pretzel and get another one free. They worked like a charm for my pre-diabetic blood sugar levels. Just what I needed to manage the weight I couldn't see.

People didn't know what to say to me so they didn't say anything at all. I don't know what was more painful, the fact that I felt like I was wearing a childless, motherless scarlet letter, or the fact that my hefty 246 lb body made me invisible. I had never been that heavy and never experienced the discrimination that goes along with carrying extra weight. Doors that used to be held open for me weren't, women who used to talk to me about fashion stopped, the second looks I used to get from men were gone, and the energy that I used to have vanished.

Then there was the weight no one could see. Behind the big giant smile was a big giant fracture. I had dated men before and felt broken-hearted, but this was different. My heart wasn't broken. My heart had been shredded. It had been torn apart beyond recognition. I wasn't in pain. I had been in pain before and this was beyond being in pain. My therapist kept saying, "Cledra, I know this must be hard." I had done hard things before, but this was beyond hard. The English language didn't have a word to describe how it felt to go from seeing a beating heart to six months of ultrasounds witnessing the destruction of your baby's body.

I remember watching Oprah and a model was talking about the tsunami she had survived and how she held on to a tree as the smell of death surrounded her and every bone in her body was breaking. She had my attention because she had come close to describing how I felt. I too had a tree… A tree of hope that I held on to, as everything in me was broken and death surrounded me. I could smell death too. The fragrance of death was strong when I'd get invitations to baby showers. The scent of death would pass me when I'd see newborns in December. It reminded me of how my baby would be a newborn. The stench of death was with me like oxygen. Every waking moment death surrounded me as I held on to my tree of hope. Then, like the model shared, she eventually let go when it was safe. Maybe that's what I was doing… Letting go of my tree of hope.

My husband was a minister and I told him I didn't want to pray anymore. My prayers obviously didn't matter to God and neither did my pain. What kind of God would torture a woman who wanted a baby so badly by making her watch the destruction of her baby, cell by cell? What kind of God would allow a woman to feel so much joy and follow that with so much devastation? NO, I didn't need or want to pray because I was convinced that it didn't work. I had been in church my entire life. I had gone through the checklist of praying, fasting, leaning on HIS word, trusting and never doubting, and I was in the middle of a tsunami, surrounded by death.

Years later, I still parent from the other side of the grave. On his EDD 12/19, I think about how tall he would be. I wonder how he'd be doing heading to kindergarten. I imagine his hugs and being in my arms telling me about his time at school. No, the mind never stops parenting a child from both sides of the grave. I wonder if he'd want the latest X-Box like other kids this year for his birthday. All those things cross my mind just like they cross the minds of every mommy, except it's a different view from the grave. In some ways we all parent from the grave. It's a series of letting go, wondering if you did everything you could, and praying with all that you have that they will be okay without you. Yes, I've learned: Once a mommy always a mommy. You never forget your baby.

The people who did know about my baby just made me sick to talk to. One of my closest friends at the time was also pregnant. It was hard to be her friend and to listen to her excitement. I know it was hard for her to be my friend also and struggle over sending the baby shower invitation or not; to stop talking about the most exciting time of her life or not; to exclude me from it all or not. Intellectually, I got that we were both struggling to love each other, but we had grown dependent on needing each other.

I remember the last day I had to go to the hospital. They said I would survive, but they had to remove the remains of my baby. I called Regina, and she said, "That's the housekeeper. I'm gonna call you right back." I needed her more in that moment than I had ever needed her, but I was trying to understand that her life was still moving forward even though mine was buried under a tsunami. I waited an hour. Nothing. Another three hours, and nothing. The resentment was flooding my mind as I recalled all the many days I had talked to Regina through IVF and through her pregnancy worries. My baby was dead and I was childless and she couldn't call me back?

I couldn't wait another minute. I texted her and wrote, "I can't believe you haven't called me back. I've listened to you and been there for you, and I really need you." Still nothing. She didn't call or return my text. I added her to the list of things that just didn't turn out the way I expected. Months went by and still nothing. My therapist said that my life to Regina was too painful to look at while she was celebrating being a mommy. That didn't comfort the loneliness I felt. My husband tried to be there for me, but there's nothing like a good girlfriend.

When you're in the darkness of a tsunami, you don't recognize the light. I decided to focus on the memorial service that the doctors and my therapist had recommended we have. Once again, I was at a loss. Should we keep some of his remains and bury them, or leave him at the hospital? That's what parents from this side of the grave think about. We think about where our baby should rest too.

I had my answer when I asked the doctor, "So just where will his body go as this medicine destroys his tissue? Will it come out of my body?" She said he would reabsorb into my body. That brought me so much comfort. He would always be in my body. That was my answer. My body would be his resting place until my life ended on this side, and then together we would rise. Yes that was the story that brought me the most comfort. Besides, I had spent years believing the dead in Christ will rise when Jesus comes back, and that was one part of my faith that I held on to. My baby would rise, but for now he would be safe with me. I decided to put all of that in a poem for his service:

Sleep tight my little angel
My heart will beat for both of us
Until Gabriel blows his trumpet and the death angel sings

On that day of glory when God opens up the skies,
you and I will go home together, because the dead in Christ shall rise

Sleep tight for now my angel and may your soul rest
Mommy is running life's race for both of us and I promise to do my very best

- Love Mommy

Something happened to me at that service. My son was in me and he was with Christ. I could feel it. I knew it and now the question was what to do with it?

I went to Women's Bible Study on Saturday mornings, mainly because the only women who could consistently make a Saturday morning Bible Study were like me. They either never had children or their children were grown and gone. I had a lot in common with the grown and gone mommies. I would listen to them talk about how their children didn't call or how they were lazy and how it was time for them to let them go. I could relate. Similar to my academic life, I was in advanced placement classes. The lessons went faster, deeper, and we moved on quickly. Yep, I got it as these gray-haired women talked about finding their way now in this chapter of their lives, "grown & gone" as a mommy. Most were also divorced or widowed.

I had found my place. No one in this crowd was talking about baby weight or when to have their next child, and it was a gift. The minister leading the group told me one Saturday something I'll never forget, after I shared the loss of my baby. She said, "Cledra, have you considered that none of this was about you? Some of us are called to teach, and there may just be something in all of this for you to teach."

TEACH WHAT? To not get your hopes up too high? To not hang your hat on marrying a man who loves the Lord? To not believe in God? I only shared it with Hershey, but my faith in God was gone. I had nothing to say to God. It was obvious to me that what I had to say didn't matter, so why continue the conversation?

But there was something about my visit to the shore of what I know was the entrance to the other side of eternity. There was something about my doctor telling me that as the medicine destroyed my baby's body that my body would reabsorb the pieces of him. Combined, those two realities haunted me. Not in a Friday the 13th haunted house way, but in a way that disturbed my spirit. In some way, as much as I had wanted to give birth to HC, that little baby that never made it to my arms had given birth to a new me. He had changed his mommy's life forever. I could feel him. I could sense him. And I knew his message to return to the shore wasn't just for me to curl up, hate God, and wait for death. There had to be more. What exactly that was, I didn't know.

I had a feeling that I was going to say again, "I can't believe this happened" and the next time it was going to bring hope to the world. Where do you go from a place of not having a clue about which way to turn? For me the answer was to run.

"Since we are surrounded by so great a cloud of witnesses, let us lay aside every weight and sin, which clings so closely, and let us run with endurance the race that is set before us." That scripture stood out to me one Sunday. In spite of hearing it all my life, it was hitting my heart this time. I still didn't have enough clarity, but what I did know was that dropping the weight would help me see things differently. My hope was that running would in some way be the windshield wipers on my foggy life.

Was my baby my witness? Was my inability and unwillingness to let go of the way life had to go in order for me to be happy the sin that was clinging so closely? What other weight did I have to let go besides the extra 80 lbs I had added to my body? I didn't know the answer, but what I did know at the end of my baby's memorial service was that I was going to run and find out for myself just what HC was trying to tell me to do back on the shore.

I signed up for a 5K race less than two weeks after the service. Yep, 3.2 miles weighing 246 lbs and with no training. It was my tribute to HC. He had brought me so much joy and, while brief, it was permanent. Joy can't be destroyed; it can only be transformed. I loved running because when I ran as fast as I could, I could feel my heart beating. There it was again: thump, thump, thump, thump. I couldn't tell the difference from the sweat and the tears, but the feeling of my heart beating was the one reminder I had of a time that brought me so much joy.

People ask me all the time how I got myself moving in such a dark time. I can sum it up in one word… Heartbeat. The gift of my baby's heartbeat is why I can run every day of my life until I feel that beat. But that's now and I need to share more about then.

PlanBE Action Steps to Drop the Weight of "I Can't Believe This Happened to Me!"

IDENTIFY:

What caused to have you say ICBTH ("I Can't Believe This Happened")?

What has this done to your faith in God, in yourself, in others?

DROP IT:

If you allowed yourself to drop the judgment of what has happened and didn't label it as good or bad, but instead made a decision to look at it as a contribution to your highest self, how would that change you and your perspective?

I KNOW the ICBTH weight is VERY difficult because, if you're like me, it could be an event that seems very unfair, makes very little sense, and seems so wrong. BUT I want to invite you to drop even the label of being unfair and also entertain the idea that understanding and moving forward don't have to be paired for progress, and that right and wrong ultimately belong to God.

REPLACE IT:

If you made the choice to turn your ICBTH event into a contribution to others, how would that look? Would it be a scholarship in honor of someone? Would it be a movement to prevent this from happening to others?Would it be a book to walk others through how you transformed your ICBTH moment?

Chapter 3:
The Weight of
"The Way It Was Supposed To BE"

The only thing more devastating than finding out your husband has been unfaithful is finding out he has been unfaithful again. You wanna know what it was about her. Why did he choose her? Was she prettier? Did she have a better body? Was she a better lover? I don't know what it is about wanting to know more details that will drive the knife deeper into your heart, but I've talked to many women about this and I wasn't alone in wanting to know it all. I think it's because when you love hard you remove all thoughts that the love you have could be anything other than the love of your life, and hearing something counter to that in a single moment doesn't erase the shell of love you've built for the person. You rationalize that the other woman couldn't possibly have something special, given what you've convinced yourself that you have.

All of that was going through my mind, especially as I held the phone and listened to my husband's mistress threaten me about coming to our home. It's like watching a movie and the credits start rolling in the middle of a beautiful scene. You think, *how can it end like this?* There must be more to it. I think that's why the desire to know more details is so strong.

This was the same year that John Edwards was caught with his mistress, and to top it off, they had conceived a child. When they said that Elizabeth Edwards ripped her blouse off in front of him, screaming, "Why don't you want me?" I understood. I overheard other women tear into her for doing that. I got it. I understood what it was like to feel unwanted by the man you had given everything you could give. I understood what it was like to take him back. Oh, I was one of those women before I got married that said with a fierce attitude, "If my man ever cheats, I'm putting him out." But that's the thing about declarations about something that you've never lived. I had lived in Elizabeth's shoes and felt her pain. I could relate to her pain. I had her pain.

Because the person you love the most has betrayed you in some ways, you question if you're also betraying yourself. Your confidence in making decisions has been shattered. As she told me how my husband had purchased a cell phone for her to use and how he would come over and play with her son, my heart sank. It made me feel like she had something I couldn't give him: A son, sex, a good time. Was I not those things?

I was hopeful we would go on and conceive again, but as I sat there holding the phone, that hope was destroyed too. My time was running out. I was approaching my late 30s and it was looking like I was also approaching divorce. Just as I was reconciling the death of my baby I was being required to reconcile the death of my marriage. I felt like I was a burn victim. You know, there's a point where you're burned so deeply you can't feel anymore.

"Well," I said to my husband's long-time mistress, "I hope that God continues to bless you and your son." That was the language of a burn victim. I couldn't hurt anymore.

It was official. My hope had been destroyed. Where were the great results that were supposed to come from working hard on my marriage? That's what I had been told. Marriage is hard work, but it's worth it. That's what I told myself when I found out about the *first* mistress. I remember calling her and asking her if she had regrets, and she adamantly said NO. But I held on to hope and hard work and for a year went to therapy and counseling, both with my husband and alone to try to be a better wife. We renewed our vows and, I thought, renewed our hope that we would be together as we had vowed twice, until death do us part.

Little did I know that we didn't stand a chance because we were never alone in our marriage. As I pulled the cell phone records I saw how my husband would leave our counseling sessions and call his mistress. I was calling on God and he was calling another woman. I always had difficulty letting go. Holding on is what I was raised to do, especially when you give your word. And I had given my word twice to love this man until the day I died.

There I was in a 5-bedroom house with an empty nursery, an empty bed, and an emptiness that I tried to fill with as much food as I could hold. It was dark in the morning and it was dark at night.

Some nights I'd go sit in the corner of my closet so that I could prop my shoulders on something. I felt that if I didn't lean against something, that I was literally going to fall through the earth.

I didn't fight for myself; I fought for my parents. I knew how shredded I felt losing a baby I never held. I couldn't imagine them feeling that kind of pain by losing me. Yes, I would fight for them, with the understanding that if they passed, then it would be fine to stop fighting. I didn't have a lot of fight left. I had made the vision boards, I had prayed, I had fasted, I had "touched and agreed", I had laid my burdens on the altar, I had done all I knew to do and yet there I was, empty and surrounded by emptiness.

I gave my Wasband most of the furniture. I just needed a bed somewhere to lay my head. And even that seemed difficult. The king-sized bed seemed to swallow me at night and so I would go to the couch and press my backside against the back so that I knew that something was holding me up on the outside even though on the inside I was shredded beyond recognition.

The saving grace was that at that time I had a job that kept me on the road. I would fly out on Sunday and return on Thursday or Friday night. It was during those flights that I met what I call my "Angels in Disguise". There was always someone who would notice my pain and in some way try to lift me up.

One Angel was a little boy who had just come from the White House. I overheard him sharing that he was so excited about having just met President Bush. I had my headphones on and as much as I tried to stay in my pity party, this little boy and his mother wouldn't stop asking me questions.

"Are you going home?"

With all that I could muster I nodded, cracked a small smile just to show enough teeth to be polite, and said, "Yes."

"Guess what?" the little boy asked.

I didn't want or feel like talking, but I indulged him and said, "What?"

"I'm dying. I have a rare cancer and I won't be here much longer. Is there anyone you want me to say 'Hello' to when I get to heaven?" The tears that were just beneath the lower lid of my eyes started to come up. "I can tell you're sad. Do you want to tell me about it?" He couldn't have been more than 10 years old.

At that point his mother intervened and said, "He does that all the time; he really is gifted."

As the tears dropped I told him, "Yes... Yes there is someone I want you to say 'Hello' to when you get to heaven..."

Before I could finish, he said, "You do know that he's here with us now don't you?" I hadn't told him my baby was a "he" but with this big bright smile my White House Angel said, "I told my mom when I'm gone I want her to finish her nursing degree so that she can help more children the way she helped me, and that's the same thing your son is telling you. You are going to help a lot of people. I love your smile and I know other people will love it too."

How could someone three feet tall be so wise? Here he was dying of a terminal illness and he was comforting *me*. He was my White House Angel. As much as I tried to ignore him, he had insisted on talking to me and now it was obvious that it was for my good and not to annoy me. As much as it hurt, it was also comforting. That's the thing about touching both sides of life at one time. There is a peace about death that comes because you know it's not a permanent end. It's just a permanent transition. My White House angel was a reminder of that.

In some strange way he knew it was time to be silent and let his message settle. It was a powerful message and one that I didn't question was from God. I looked at his mother and I could see in her eyes the joy and the sorrow. Joy that God would choose her to be a vehicle to usher such light into the world, but sorrow from the awareness that every parent eventually faces… The light doesn't belong to us. It's just passing through.

"Welcome to Charlotte, where the local time is 8 pm. Thank you for flying with us." The flight was over and my White House Angel waved at me one last time as he got his things to get off the plane. His flight was really just beginning.

Usually landings were difficult for me because there's that point when the plane lands and it's okay to get your cell phone out. In those moments I was surrounded by "Honey, I just landed" conversations or "Can't wait to see you" bubbly tones, and I would once again be reminded that there wouldn't be anyone waiting for me at home. No one was waiting to pick me up. No one was waiting for me so we could go to dinner. It was hard, but on this flight my White House Angel had made landing a little bit softer.

I didn't usually check a bag, but on this flight I had, and to my surprise my White House Angel was at baggage claim, still smiling and looking like he was about to celebrate. As he and his mom grabbed their bag, he said, "Hey lady… Look for the frogs."

"What?"

"Look for the frogs, because they're a sign… A sign from God."

His mom interjected, "Frog is his term for, Forever Rely On God. He learned that in the hospital and he shares that with people." Again, I partially smiled and said thank you.

Look for the frogs… Okay my Angel. I'll do that. I mean if he can look for frogs, so can I. At least for the rest of this night.

After that comment I made up my mind to end my pity party, grab my bags, and take myself to the movies. My Wasband and I used to go to the movies all the time and I enjoyed it. But, like everything in divorce, what you used to enjoy becomes covered in thorns. Touching it makes you bleed from the memories of what used to be. But tonight I was going to go to the movies with myself.

I called my mom to let her know I had made it back safely. My mother was the only one who faithfully called me every day. I knew she ached for me and as much as I wanted to be kind and thankful for her checking in, I fell short of showing up that way for every call. All I could do was pray that my mother understood my sometimes-snappy tone and desire to hurry off the phone.

The house was so loud with silence as I walked in and turned off the alarm. The loudest alarm was my pain. If only that came with a four-digit code to stop it from going off. That would be nice, but it wasn't happening. But I had made a vow to take myself on a date. Me, myself, and I were going to the movies, and so I forced myself to change clothes and make a quick U-turn to the movies.

As I walked up the sidewalk sandwiched between couples holding hands and families with children rushing to get inside, I saw something in the shadows. I stepped out of the current of people to look closer, and I couldn't believe what I was seeing. There on the sidewalk, as if it had been waiting for me, was a frog. I stood there as he hopped in front of me, paused for a moment, and then hopped back into the shadows.

"Look for the frogs." Just that quickly my White House Angel's words had shown up in my life. A frog on the sidewalk heading to the movies? Had they always been there and I just hadn't noticed? I couldn't help but smile. God was with me. My baby was with me. I had to get out of my own pity to see both of them. My time crying over the way it was supposed to be had been blocking me from seeing the F.R.O.G.s.

I had convinced myself that moving forward wasn't possible. Pain can do that to you. It can make you feel like you're in quicksand and, despite your attempts to save yourself, you feel like you're sinking. In seeing the frog, I realized that wasn't true. As much as I felt like I was sinking, I needed to move forward instead of focusing on stepping repeatedly in the same spot.

Nightly, I would mentally rehearse and reWHINE the events of my life: The moment my Wasband told me he was seeing someone else, followed by hearing the phone ring as the other woman called our home, followed by visions of him packing his things. It was like a record that skipped, repeating the same line again and again, and because I was in such disbelief and shock, I just sat there and let the record play over and over.

But my White House Angel had taught me something valuable. And seeing the frog so quickly after my flight couldn't have been a coincidence. However, the question still remained that I couldn't answer, and that was, HOW do I move forward? All of the books I read talked about "if it wasn't for my children I wouldn't have made it through my divorce". I didn't have a child to motivate me to get up. Or, "if it wasn't for my sisters I wouldn't have made it through." Well I was an only child and my family was three hours away. I couldn't relate to their path out of darkness, and the worst books were those that seemed to gloss over the devastation. The writer was too quick to talk about how they put it behind them. I could tell those books were written from a point of complete recovery.

Where was the book that met me in the dark? Where was the book that met me sleeping on the couch or sitting in my closet in the corner? My White House Angel had shown me that I was the book. He had spoken the frogs into my life and he had spoken that I would help a lot of people. I believed him – in that moment I believed him. I needed to answer that question of HOW… And so PlanBE was conceived. I needed to return to the moment when I was just an idea in the mind of God. The question wasn't HOW; the question was, "What did God have in mind to send to the world in a package that was now me? What purpose did the great creator want to fulfill on this earth when he allowed me to breathe life?" That was what I needed to align with and that would be the ticket in… The ticket inside of my purpose and my passion. I stopped asking God how or why and instead, I began my mornings by emptying my will and myself.

"God I'm still attached to the way things were supposed to be, but I'm willing to surrender that attachment to you. Show me the steps to replace my attachment. I'm angry and

I'm hurt, but in this moment I'm willing to find joy. Show me the steps to joy."

As I repeated my prayer to God every day, the veil started to lift. I began to see what I was supposed to do. God showed me that my birth date – 8:28 in the book of Romans – was the foundation of my life: "For we know (not think or assume) that all things (not some things) work together for good for those called according to HIS purpose" - Romans 8:28. It was my birth date and the birth right of everyone allowed to breathe another day. That became crystal clear to me.

I soon realized that I had the order all wrong. I had been giving God my list and praying for the things on my list to come true when God wanted me to seek him and wait to receive the list. My life wasn't something I could run and dictate every twist and turn and outcome. My life was an extension of God's will and the power of that extension cord was rooted in my willingness to surrender to the original purpose.

So did that mean that my baby's heart stopping was good? I discovered that the answer depended on a return to PlanBE. How willing was I to seek the idea God had in mind? I realized that my willingness or unwillingness determined whether the final conclusion would be "good". Was it possible that my son was sacrificed so that I would give birth to a movement? Was it possible that my Wasband confessed his infidelity so that we both could be free to love in integrity? Was it possible to remove judgment of right and wrong and conclude without it making sense that my baby's heart stopping was good? It was all possible, but incredibly difficult to grasp. That revelation was the glimpse God was giving me as I surrendered every morning.

I remember crying uncontrollably while watching a sermon on forgiveness and it was as if God was speaking to me himself. I was screaming, "God why are you doing this to me?" and the reply was, "I'm not doing this to you... You are doing this to you."

How was I doing this to me? The reality punched me in the face that it was my insisting that this marriage work that was hurting me. It was my insistence on making my husband someone he wasn't that was hurting me. It was my insistence that he was my only option that was hurting me. It was my belief that I could never love again this deeply that was hurting me. That is what God was trying to tell me. It was my refusal to look at what else could be happening that was causing me so much pain.

The truth was that I felt like a failure. Because I had never failed at anything in my life I didn't want to let my marriage go. I didn't even date divorced men when I was single. I made naive conclusions about the way marriage should go and that if you did everything right, then there would not be a reason to divorce. I lived my life so much like marching orders on some to-do list that I didn't allow for the will of God to have any input to create other possibilities. In ways, I was a Christian snob. People who were divorced were flawed and didn't follow the right checklist. With that tape playing in my mind I held on to the fragments of the marriage until the edges were so sharp that the choice to hold on was a choice to die. It would be a death of my integrity, esteem, and the most tragic – a death to my purpose for my life.

There was something for me on the other side of divorce, but my snobby conclusions stopped me from even entertaining what that might be until that moment when I know God spoke to my spirit. It was heart language not verbal language. It gave me a knowing that is indescribable.

I got myself together and I made an appointment with a divorce attorney. A woman in North Carolina had just settled a case for over a million dollars under the new law "alienation of affection". Basically, she sued the mistress and her husband, and won. Sitting in front of the attorney, I knew he was a pit bull. The first thing he said was, "We can easily go for a million, maybe more. You'll get most of his 401K and the business he named after you." My husband had started a company that had my initials. My mother even did the logo and the business was doing really well.

But there was something about this pit bull that turned me off. He wasn't even looking at me. He was looking at my assets on paper and chopping them up like they were wood chips for a fire that I could tell he wanted to burn really hot. *He* wanted to stick it to my husband and make a statement. But that's the thing about slinging mud. It's impossible to sling it without it getting all over you in the process.

I thanked the pit bull for his time and I took my wood chips back. I had made a commitment before God to love my husband and while that love wasn't going to be in holy matrimony, I would have a holy divorce. I didn't have any examples of how to do that, but I had plenty to tell me how it wasn't done.

So, for starters, I didn't hire the pit bull. I knew that was a good first step. There was a part of my ego that tingled at the idea of suing his mistress, but it was fleeting. Once I got back home I just went to my usual corner of my closet and sat there and cried. "God help me," is all I could manage to say.

The next day I met with Laura Hatcher, ESQ. She was a petite little power-house and at first I thought, was she the female pit bull equivalent? Until she opened our conversation with, "So how are you? Would you like some coffee?" I felt like she was looking at me and not at my assets. There was a person behind the big house, the big business, and the possibility of the big settlement and Laura got that in the first few seconds. I told her I was broken and lost, but that I knew I had to move forward with a divorce. She reached for my hand and said, "I'll do what I can to get you through this." And she kept her word.

My divorce was as loving as I could make it. Even Laura said that it was the most pleasant divorce she had ever represented. That had been my goal. In some ways I felt that if I could figure out how to only hold love in my hand, then love is what I would have to offer moving forward. I didn't know when that day would come, but I knew that holding on to bitterness, anger, resentment, and hostility the way I had seen so many others handle divorce wasn't going to be for me. No, I would do my divorce my way and on my terms and that meant with love. My vows now were between me and God and God had over 2,000 years of proof that HE kept his promises. Now it was my turn. Love would stand by my side as I signed the divorce papers. Forgiveness is what I'd hold in my mind and a focus on surrendering to God's will is what I would wake up to every morning moving forward. Those were my vows until death do us part… But now, the vow was between God and me.

PlanBE Action Steps to Drop the Weight of "The Way It Was Supposed to BE"

IDENTIFY:

Identify the areas in your life where you are insisting, forcing, and literally arguing daily with the idea that there can only BE one way?

What is your insistence costing you?

DROP IT:

Write the following: "I am willing to surrender… (place what you identified here) …for the next 24 hours. At the end of those 24 hours I am free to take the weight back, but until that time I invite the power of God to show me what else is possible as a result of (what you identified) taking place."

REPLACE IT:

Take the feelings that go along with insisting your life go a certain way and create a list of the opposite. So for example, here are some of the feelings I was experiencing:

- I felt like I was a failure because my marriage failed.

- I felt like I must've been missing something for my Wasband to be unfaithful.

- I felt like I wasn't as valuable as a woman because I wasn't a mother.

My "replace the weight" list looked like this:

- I'm courageous, not a failure, to leave a marriage that doesn't honor who I am.

- My Wasband had a choice to communicate with me instead of cheat on me. I'm not missing anything.

- God determined my value at birth and not being a mother doesn't diminish God's appraisal.

You get the point? Challenge your beliefs about what you have identified and I promise you will start to replace the weight of "the way it was supposed to be".

So what about you? What are you holding in your hand? Don't answer too quickly before you rewind the tape of your life. Are you blaming someone else for what you haven't been able to accomplish in your life? Are you arguing with a reality that you refuse to accept?

What was "supposed to be" by now in your life?

What did that NOT happening cost you in your life?

Chapter 4:

The Weight of a Struggling Goodbye

"Chippy if you're gonna hang around a long time you're gonna have to get good at saying goodbye."

Those were the words of my paternal grandfather as I stood beside him after the funeral services for one of his sisters. He was one of 15 children born to my paternal great grandparents, and his journey would include having to say goodbye to 12 of his siblings, two sons, and a wife before the day would come for me to say goodbye to him. Because my life had not required me to say goodbye that often, I didn't understand what my grandfather meant. For me, saying goodbye to my dear German Shepherd had been the most painful thing I had experienced. Jake was like a brother to me and I talked to him just like I would any person, without any regard to the fact that he was a dog. So for me, life was full of a lot of peaks and very few valleys. Little did I know that the reason life had so few goodbyes was only because I hadn't lived very much life.

The year I got engaged I had the same expectancy for life to be full of a lot of peaks. After all, I was one of the last of my friends to find "the one" to spend the rest of my life with, so I felt somewhat entitled to having all joy. But shortly after I threw myself into planning a very large wedding of my dreams, my grandfather was diagnosed with esophageal cancer. I was standing beside him when they said that he would never eat or drink again in his life. As shocking as the doctor's comments were to me, my grandfather's response was equally shocking. He said, "Okay," and then asked me to wheel him outside so he could hear the birds and see the sky. I knew it was also to smoke a cigarette.

It was mind boggling that he could hold that news with so much emotional indifference. Everything about his response suggested he was in a place of complete acceptance. As I wheeled him outside the hospital, I couldn't help but rewind to another time we were in the hospital together. Granddaddy had been cutting grass around a pond and the tractor turned over on him. I met him and my father at the Emergency Room only to find my grandfather sitting with his long legs crossed, again with emotional indifference and complete acceptance. I, on the other hand, paced back and forth and demanded that he be seen immediately. He just looked at me with a partial smile and said, "They'll get to me when they can. You may as well sit down."

But sitting down was the last thing I was willing to do. I paced, I ate, and I worried, all while Granddaddy was still waiting for his name to be called on their time and their terms. When they finally got to him they said, "Mr. McCullers, your left lung is almost completely collapsed. Are you feeling okay?"

Once again with emotional indifference, he said, "Yes, I'm fine." His oxygen use was at a level so low the nurse said that it was amazing that he was sitting there so calmly. His gaze was fixed on the outside, looking at the birds and looking at the sky. At that time a disposition of acceptance and a willingness to sit in pain made me angry. I wanted him to fight. I wanted him to tell them they had taken too long because life hadn't put me in a hard enough corner where the only way out was through the door of acceptance.

Life hadn't balanced my beliefs enough back then for me to understand or even appreciate the lessons Granddaddy was teaching me without saying a word. He was a man who had served in World War II, lost two children, buried his wife, and watched double-digit siblings be buried in the family cemetery. Some character traits are only born from tragedy, and because I hadn't experienced anything that was beyond my ability to change using either my intellect or my contacts, I was still in a place of fighting instead of flowing with life's inevitable goodbye moments.

So as I rolled Granddaddy outside to look at the sky and see the birds, all I felt was anger; anger that this news of my grandfather's cancer would happen when it was supposed to be a happy time in my life. I had finally found the man of my dreams, was in the middle of planning a mega wedding, and now I was going to have to tell my father that his father had a terminal illness. My mind wrestled with how unfair it was for my family to not have complete joy during this time. At that point, life hadn't broken me to the point of surrendering to a plan other than my own and so my default was to fight and to do it full of anger.

My wedding was just a few months away and according to the doctors my grandfather wasn't going to make it. I felt like a dark cloud surrounded what was supposed to be a happy time. After Granddaddy finished his cigarette and got enough of the birds and sky watching, we went back in for him to check in to his room. In silence he just flowed with the entire check-in process until the doctor came into the room again. That's when he started to talk back with what seemed like an emotional shift. He told the doctor that he already had his tuxedo for my wedding and that it was expensive and so he would be around at least until my wedding. Emotionally conflicted, I smiled while my eyes filled with tears. How could he predict that? Was he right? He said it with so much conviction that I wanted to believe him. But my awareness of the unmerciful assault cancer can have sent me spiraling on the inside. It was all just so unfair.

The doctor asked if he could speak with me for a moment outside. My mind started racing again. What else could this one day hold for me to hear? "You know, I have seen people who have something they're looking forward to be the reason they survive, so it's great that you're getting married," the doctor confided in me. I didn't know what to say, think, or feel in that moment, but I managed to give a partial smile and say thanks. All I could wonder was how my father was going to handle all of this? My father and I were alike in that we were fighters. If I could guess my father's response, it would be silence followed by a fight to do everything known to man to help my grandfather survive. But it did cross my mind just how would I handle my grandfather not making it to my wedding? My mind and my emotions were racing off track right into the ditch of predicting doom and gloom.

Fast-forward several months. Granddaddy's prediction came true. He was too weak to walk, but he came to my wedding wearing the tuxedo he had paid for just days before his diagnosis. I could tell he was using everything he had left to make it for my special day. He was never a large man and didn't have a lot of weight to lose, but the cancer was starting to outmatch his will.

His health declined rapidly after my wedding. My aunt called to me tell me he wasn't doing well and that the doctor thought he was in his final days. I took the day off and drove three hours to sit with him in the hospital. Looking into his pretty, hazel, almond-shaped eyes, I could tell he wasn't looking back anymore. He was fading. My maternal grandfather used to talk about the "death rattle" people get in the final hours of life. As I looked at him and listened to his breathing more carefully, I wondered if that's what I was hearing. Was that his death rattle? Was I in the presence of the Angel of Death? I can't explain why, but I couldn't stop watching him. There's something about knowing the final hour is near that makes you want to soak up every single second. I didn't want him to feel like he was alone, and so I sat as he looked through me. After almost eight hours of watching, I decided to drive home. I hugged him for what I knew would be the last time and left the hospital.

I was half-way home when a flock of birds surrounded my car at the same time my cell phone rang. "Cledra he's gone. He just passed away." I stared out my windshield looking at the sky and the birds, just as I had that first day of his diagnosis, and I knew in that moment it wasn't a coincidence; the birds were a sign from Granddaddy that he was okay. He had flown away and was where he loved to be – outside with the birds and the sky. As much as I wanted him to have company on his last day, I realized there is a moment for all of us when our body's purpose has expired, and all of the physical comforts we once needed, including companionship, are no longer needed or desired. My grandfather was looking through me on that last day because he was crossing the bridge from this world to eternity. It was his final goodbye.

The next time I saw him was to prepare for his home-going service at the funeral home. As sad as my body felt, my spirit was at peace because I knew he was at peace. All was well because he welcomed his goodbye in order to say hello to his next chapter in eternity. But truthfully, the only way I reached peace over his death was because he was almost 90 years old, so I told myself that made it all right. There was a part of me that could accept that it was okay to say goodbye after a life lived fully.

I still didn't grasp the whole notion of flowing instead of fighting life at that point, nor did I really understand the value of having a profound goodbye, unless there was a rational, logical reason like being 90. At the funeral, I stared more at my father than my grandfather. I wondered how he was holding the pain of losing his father. And then I wondered how I would ever hold that same pain. I had watched both of my parents bury their mothers and the idea of losing my mother was unbearable to even imagine. Newly married, I hung all of my hope on the idea that I had a chance to create my own family. That day brought me face-to-face with the fact that family I had known my entire life would some day expire. The time would come when everyone I had the privilege to know from birth to adulthood wouldn't walk with me into my senior years. That's the thing about saying goodbye to the dead. It highlights your own mortality and the cycle of life that isn't optional for any of us.

Due to my stubborn nature, in spite of all of the wonderful enlightenment from my grandfather's death, I returned to fighting life instead of flowing.

It wouldn't be until what I call my emotional tsunami that I truly understood and embraced what my grandfather was trying to say. The day I had come face-to-face with my baby on a giant flat screen, his body magnified by what seemed like a trillion times so that I could clearly see that his heart had stopped, was the day I began my life course in dropping the weight of goodbye. It was, and honestly continues to be, the most difficult to learn, and more importantly to put into consistent action.

I share that so that you can give yourself the gift of patience. Impatience is an indicator that you still want to fight instead of surrender. This weight, like all of the weights in this book, doesn't come with a "read it and you're done" guarantee. I invite you to see this more as a practice, that you choose to repeat as life demands you to drop additional weight. No one is getting out of life alive or without scars, but I hope in some way this practice helps you to let go without the additional pain that can come from refusing to flow.

Before I get to the steps to drop the weight of struggling with goodbye I want to visit some of the *reasons* we struggle with goodbye. There are three beliefs that go along with struggling with goodbye:

1. a belief that life can be controlled

2. a belief that you're entitled to fairness

3. a belief that a great fight will eventually lead to a great outcome

These beliefs are the fertilizer that feeds our refusal to accept that it's time to say goodbye. And so we struggle. We struggle because with the fertilizer that life can be controlled instead of saying goodbye, we spend time online looking at Google researching, believing that the right combination of information is out there and once we find it then we can control and ultimately change the outcome.

When the oncologists were saying there was nothing else they could do to prolong my grandfather's life, I went online and researched different herbs and alternative treatments to cancer. I called all of the physicians I knew from my previous job to get their opinion. I exhausted myself with an insistence of my will and a refusal to accept that the physical expiration date for my grandfather had come.

When we feel entitled to fairness, we struggle, because instead of saying goodbye, we spend our time focused on all the good we have done and how that means we have earned the right for life to give us what we want as a reward for all of our good works. For me, I didn't even realize I had an entitlement belief until the death of my baby. I felt like I had taken my time to marry a man who was successful, build a career, and build a home with a great in-law suite and nursery, and set up life in the order that would in return allow me to have my family. I was clueless that I had a quid pro quo approach to life. *I do this, and in exchange, Universe, you obey and give me my just due.* Entitlement is a sneaky belief because it can masquerade as a good belief system, when in fact it isn't, and it isn't discovered or revealed until crap hits the fan and plans get jacked up. That is when you find out if entitlement has been playing in the background.

In my experience with my own life and with working with many clients, no one readily admits to entitlement. It's when life gets in your face that most people get real about what's holding them back.

It was my belief that I was entitled that also brought me face-to-face with the God I had believed in all my life. I realized I didn't have the mature belief system I thought I had, but instead I had a childlike "Santa Claus" God. It was a "naughty or nice" belief system, that if I was, in my opinion, nice, then God would give me a nice life. If I was naughty, then I could repent and again return to the life I was entitled to have. The idea that I was created with the single purpose to become more like my creator for the sake of my creator's plan was a foreign concept. So keep that in mind as you practice this idea of dropping the weight of goodbye, and challenge yourself to evolve past a "Santa Claus" God.

The last belief that fertilizes our inability to say goodbye is that a great fight will create a great outcome. This belief usually comes with a bad attitude, a lot of anger, and resentment that could fill a cruise ship. The bad attitude is a result of an increased effort not resulting in increased results. The anger comes from the mounting frustration from doing work that seems so logical, only to continue to get an illogical outcome. And finally, the cruise ship of resentment often comes from comparing our effort to others who got the outcome we desire and yet we're not getting the same results.

My cruise ship of resentment started sailing when every single person on my sales team had a baby over a two-year period, while I was recovering from affairs and miscarriages. I was resentful that their marriages hadn't been ravaged by the storms of infidelity. I was angry that their pregnancies went to term without any complications. And when I listened to what they were doing and it was the same thing I had done during my pregnancy, the cruise ship set sail in high speed. It seemed like at every turn people were doing the same thing I was doing and getting the results I wanted, and yet I had to watch my results fall short again and again.

Because I hadn't allowed myself to believe that my outcome had nothing to do with my direct efforts or lack of effort, I couldn't see that the plan that God put in place when he created me looked very different from the plan I was insisting and forcing to come true. The thread of surrender is required in order to weave a great goodbye with the ability to cover the coldness of life not going as planned. I will warn you that feelings of sadness and overwhelm are very common when you decide to create new beliefs around a great goodbye.

Grief is another required thread because surrendering your belief in the way you thought your life would be is a loss. But do not allow yourself to believe that because you're losing the way you thought life would be that you're also losing the ability to have a great life. That is a lie that will whisper to you as you surrender. But know that it is only fear masquerading as fact as you shift from fighting to flowing.

Now that you have an idea of the beliefs that are beneath the struggle to say goodbye, let's move into how to actually drop the weight of struggling with goodbye.

I have identified four steps. The first and the most challenging is to surrender to the idea that what you had planned and what God had planned may in fact be two different things. At first this shifted my anger from the situation to anger at God. I just couldn't wrap my mind around the idea that the loving God that I believed in would allow my baby's heart to stop, allow me to carry him for six months, all to save my uterus so that I could go on to try to have another baby, only for my marriage to fall apart and for me to never get the chance to try to conceive again in my marriage. How could God have allowed such a horrible sequence of events and call that love?

After a lot of time meditating, where I would picture myself giving God my will and my plans, it was revealed to me that the sequence of events included free will on my husband's part, and on mine. I used my free will to fight to not have the recommended hysterectomy. I used my free will to take my husband back after the first affair, believing it would be the last. My husband used his free will to invite other women into our marriage during my pregnancy. My husband used his free will to not tell me the truth as we renewed our vows and promised each other we would move forward without looking back, knowing it was a lie. We cannot underestimate the impact of free will on the sequence of events.

Now let me add that there are times when free will has absolutely nothing to do with the outcome. The person who has a massive heart attack or aneurysm didn't participate in the outcome. There are no absolutes, because when we surrender, we are also surrendering to the need to have life make sense.

Another thread to include is to surrender your logic. We must grow to accept that we will not understand or be able to make sense of everything that happens in our lives. Some situations will remain a mystery and we must evolve to a point to live our purpose in the mystery. The supernatural will never make natural sense; otherwise it wouldn't be supernatural. Surrendering requires submitting to the fact that we are an extension of the Almighty and the Almighty isn't just on standby to meet our every request. Sometimes we can treat God like an on-demand movie channel, with a belief that when we press a certain button it's time to play.

After the big bite of surrender is taken, the next step is to accept. Accept the reality of your life as is and as if nothing will change. I know this may seem counter to what most books will tell you, but in my experience, accepting things as is allows us to give up the fighting, the Google searches, the researching, the endless obsessing, and the worrying.

I would spend hours picturing myself by a stream where I would put my hopes into the water and watch them float away. Other times I would write my hopes on an index card and attach it to a balloon and then watch it ascend to the sky. It was my way of declaring that I was surrendering and accepting, that I no longer controlled my life or the circumstances or even the hopes of my life. This is a critical step because accepting life as is, with an accompanying belief that nothing will change, allows mental liberation. In that liberation, you will free space for new possibilities that were previously occupied by struggle and worry.

The next step is to take new action. Note that I said new action. For most of us, we have been busy, but we haven't been effective. Many confuse the two concepts and are exhausted to no avail. This step requires you to fill your mind with something new.

To take another page from my life, I moved into new action by asking myself why did I want to create a family of my own in the first place? Why had it been so important for me to have children? The answer was that I had been given the tremendous gift of great parents, great grandparents, great aunts and uncles, who all filled my life with love and life lessons. I didn't want those lessons to die when my life ended. I wanted a family and a child so that I could have a legacy. So the next question was for me to ask how could I create that legacy in other ways than being a mother or a wife? It wasn't until I created space as a result of the mental liberation that comes from surrender that my mind started to give me ideas about creating a legacy in the absence of having a biological family. And you are holding one of the answers. You and I may never meet, but the lessons you take from this book will outlive me. The goal of the life lessons being passed on has been met. You are, in fact, a part of the legacy I had hoped to have in giving birth. So, welcome to my family!

So ask your self, what are the other possible ways you could reach the goal you had in mind? Ask a different question with an open mind to receive directions to take a new path, and I promise you the answers will amaze you!

In the darkest moments, as I struggled to learn how to say goodbye, the books I read only added to my anger because most of them included details of how the author ultimately got exactly what they wanted on their terms. Those books were written by women who claimed they grew spiritually, but ultimately were about how they got remarried and went on to have children. I wanted to read about a happy outcome after the possibility of having the life you wanted has been destroyed. I wanted to read the book about the woman who didn't get the happy ending she was hoping for and yet she somehow found a way to create a happy beginning. I wanted an answer to the question of how to be happy when you have the wisdom to do things differently, but your time to do it differently is over. My time to have a happy first marriage was over, and my struggle to recover was beginning. I wanted a blueprint of how to make that happen. That blueprint didn't exist. And so I created it.

I still remember the first morning I woke up and my pillow was dry. I was so happy. I wondered if my body would ever stop crying involuntarily in my sleep. And when it did, I got busy taking notes. I wanted to share the way out.

That leads me to the final step to overcome struggling to say goodbye, and that is to have a funeral. Have a funeral for your unmet dreams. Write those dreams on beautiful stationary, and be creative. Invite your closest friends or you can choose to have it alone, but it's important to honor your loss with a service to finalize it all. I had a funeral service for the man I thought I married, the man who would never cheat on me, would always tell me the truth no matter how hard, and we would go on to have a family together. I had to bury that man because he passed away.

I had a funeral service for my dream of being a mother. The entire way I saw my life playing out was forever changed and, in fact, it too had passed away.

Like all funeral services this step comes with all of the stages of grief, so don't expect a feeling of relief right away. This is a necessary part of your journey because in its absence we continue the fight with life and never enter the flow of life. It is only in the flow that we evolve into our highest self because we are being ushered by the Almighty and not by our will. When we say goodbye, supernatural events start taking place to elevate us in every area of our life. But it requires going through the dark night of the funeral.

I can't emphasize enough the importance of being patient with yourself and with those around you as you drop the weight of a struggling goodbye. You may find yourself a little on edge or snappy as you take these steps, and please know this is normal. I would also like to caution you against isolating during this time. Get a coach or a therapist or both to assist you through this step.

While saying goodbye can ultimately be liberating, the path to that liberation is punctuated with a lot of emotional potholes. Some to be aware of would be pity, wallowing, numbing behavior like over- or under-eating or excessive shopping, experimenting with drugs, or promiscuity. There's a reason the cliché "to get over someone old get under someone new" exists. Many who are going through a divorce numb the pain through promiscuity.

Be gentle and be kind to yourself and give yourself the gift of inviting someone into your process. Please don't underestimate the potholes or the emotional avalanche that can occur on the path to saying goodbye.

Start every morning by setting your intention to surrender. Remember, this is a practice and so you must recommit daily. This is a Morning Surrender Prayer that I use that I hope will support you in beginning each day with a posture of surrender.

Morning Surrender

My eyes are open for yet another day
Lord let me recognize your will and only your way

I empty my plans and surrender them to you
For the next 24 hours your will is all I want to do

Open my heart and mind to look for you in everyone I meet
Let your goodness and mercy flow from my head to the bottom of my feet

When another day ends in this finite life of mine
I thank you in advance for all you did and didn't do in this period of time

So as I get up and put my feet on the floor
I know that everything is as it should be and I ask you for nothing more.

~ Your goodbye companion

While this prayer is a morning prayer please use it at any time of the day. I cannot emphasize enough the importance of allowing yourself time to embrace the skills to dropping the weight of goodbye. Know that I am with you on the journey and invite you to reach out to me for additional support if needed.

Chapter 5:
The Weight of Excess Body Weight

Excess weight is like a tiny drip in a faucet. At first no one notices, but then the entire floor is soaked and it becomes urgent to change it. Anyone who has struggled with weight can relate. It's like months or sometimes years can pass and the slow, steady gain is unnoticed. It's passed off as the cleaner's shrinking the clothes, or the cut and style changing by the same designer from one year to the next, or maybe it's the forgiving elastic waist wardrobe. At any rate, it's usually some culminating event that makes us say, "I have had it. This weight has to go". It's the point where all the reasons you've used to do nothing become unacceptable and even the argument that the camera angle was bad becomes void. Then, you end up moving the bar for what's unacceptable until you reach a weight where you just don't even recognize yourself anymore.

My first unacceptable weight was 135 lbs. I remember it like it was yesterday, even though it was over 30 years ago. Mr. Allen said it was time for the Presidential Fitness Test, but first we had to get weighed. I always cringed because at 11 years old and already 5'9" tall, I had no chance of being in the weight range of the girls who were 4'11" or the boys who were 5'2" tall. It seemed illogical to expect to weigh the same, but in an 11-year old mind, where being just like everyone else reigns supreme to winning the lottery, to weigh more than the boys even though they were a ½ foot shorter was an unacceptable weight. Sure enough, as Mr. Allen moved the scale to 135 lbs the dwarfs in my class started singing, "Don't wanna bump with that big fat woman" as they surrounded the scale looking at my weight. And those that didn't sing made moo sounds just to cement the idea that I was bigger than everyone else.

Seeing the tears about to jump over the bottom lid of my eyes, Mr. Allen said, "You just wait Cledra. These boys are gonna be all over you in a few years." IN A FEW YEARS? Was that supposed to be consolation? I didn't care about in a few years. I needed some advice that would get me through lunchtime without rewinding cow sounds and the latest R&B song about bumping a big fat woman. That did nothing to stop the floodgates of tears and the shame I felt at that moment about being me.

Looking back through my now 42-year old lens, I know without a doubt, that is the moment I attached shame to showing up just as I am, and at the same time assigned a label that I wasn't good enough. The message was enforced every Valentine's Day at school when these same dwarfs would give me a card that had some large animal, which varied year to year from a pig, to an elephant, to a hippopotamus. Inside the card would always be some version of how I went over big with them. I don't know why I tortured myself with hope every year that maybe one year I'd open a card that included a sincere admission that I was beautiful enough to be one of the dwarf's girlfriend.

So that summer I went on my first diet. I read my mom's Weight Watcher material and I was determined to drop below 100 lbs just like everyone else. It was equivalent to saying I would only breathe every other day all summer. I was destined to fail, but even at 11 I was determined and convinced that anything was possible. I mean, that's what it said in the Bible right?

By the end of the summer I wasn't below 135 lbs. In fact, the unhealthy restrictive dieting gave me a brand new skill set – binge eating. I was up to 165 lbs. I also added another inch to my height so I returned taller and being even further away from dwarf weight.

But my creative juices came up with a plan for my last year in middle school. I got my mom to write a note that included my weight from the doctor and then I cleverly altered the weight. I guess Mr. Allen remembered the water works from the year before and just accepted my obviously altered note that said, "Please excuse Cledra from weighing. She weighs 95 lbs and is currently 5'10" tall." Only a man who had daughters could relate to my need to get away with this kind of fantasy, and Mr. Allen just let it go.

By this point I had shame, was not feeling good enough, binge eating, and lying about my weight as new coping skills to deal with my womanly figure at age 12. I was perfectly poised and positioned to soak up additional ineffective skills as I headed into high school. The dwarfs grew over the summer heading into high school, so being tall was becoming less and less the exception and the animal kingdom Valentine's Day cards stopped.

Because my mother was a teacher at the high school I was assigned to, she thought I would have a better chance socially if I went to a different school. It was like a clean slate for me. All I could hope was that there were fewer dwarfs at the new high school and more tall boys and girls like me. But because I was being bused from rural North Carolina into the city for the new high school, I had to ride the short bus. The short bus took off major cool points because everyone laughed at the way it looked. All I could think was, *Great. Now I not only arrive in a bus that looks ridiculous I may tower over everyone and be headed into another animal kingdom celebration.* And as if that wasn't enough, I had just had braces added to my already awkward appearance. Back then they didn't have cute rubber bands to match your outfit or the different color brackets. No, they had the heavy-duty metal brackets with rubber bands that felt like someone was pulling back on your head like you were a horse saddled for a long ride. The bracket technology wasn't refined like it is now and you talked funny and all "s" words came with a lot of spit. It was disgusting, but my parents must have taken a page from Mr. Allen and constantly said, "IN A FEW YEARS you're gonna be happy". I was always curious why there wasn't an "in a few *days*" option, but there never was, at least not when it came to braces and my weight.

Looking back now, I know my parents and Mr. Allen were just telling me the truth. The truth was that my issue of drastically outgrowing everyone *was* going to take years for others to catch up. The truth was that my large overbite with my teeth and the giant space between my teeth *was* going to take years to correct. There was no easy way to say it, so I guess they just resorted to "in a few years" you're gonna be happy about this. And today the irony is that I get complimented the most on my smile when someone meets me for the first time, and my first book is all about weight. I guess I have the dwarfs and the animal kingdom to thank.

Beyond my smile and my book, I wanted to bring up a little of my childhood issues around weight because I now know that's where the drive for external validation and a sense of belonging came from, and that because the external dwarfs change if we put our motives outside of ourselves, we never lose the weight with an internal motive that's constant, but one that is constantly changing. This shows up in adults in the form of losing weight for an event, or for a season. On the surface it seems benign, but on a deeper level it's a malignant approach to weight that trades building a healthy life for building a matrix of quick fix habits that ultimately create a sliding scale of additional toxic behavior. Behaviors like starving, over exercising, obsessing, eating disorders, and compulsive overeating are born from weight loss goals that focus on time instead of the best life. Our best life comes one day at a time and the present moment is an opportunity full of possibility. A certain weight by a certain date makes the present an inconvenience, something to hurry through because tomorrow has the illusion of being better than today. The problem is that even tomorrow becomes a waste if the scale doesn't line up with the time frame that has been predetermined.

I stayed in this toxic cycle for years. Having meltdowns over slight gains from week to week, ignoring the idea that to fluctuate by 1-2 lbs is normal, especially for a woman. It also played out emotionally where it was a good day if the scale was down and a bad day if it was up. The seeds planted by the dwarfs took root and for many years I allowed the way they made me feel – inadequate, less than, estranged, and not enough – to be the motivation for taking care of myself. And those toxic seeds produced lethal fruit that I would dine on for all of my 20s and 30s.

I went from program to program. Every magazine article that had the hint of a "secret" to solve my weight problem was purchased. Every year when Weight Watchers ran a special promoting their new program, I was the first to join. Every January I was purchasing new gym clothes, buying new workout videos, and stocking my fridge with the latest combination that promised freedom from my lethal fruit.

Looking back, I have to say that all of the programs worked. The problem is that they focused on the physical weight and never challenged me to dig up the toxic roots that continued to feed the lethal fruit that fed my yo-yo weight cycles, my binge eating, my poor financial investments in memberships, and my constantly believing there was just something about me that if I could fix I could eliminate the weight problem that had plagued my life. The constant attack of my weight from the outside slowly destroyed my belief in myself on the inside. After two decades of believing and hoping and working out, only to have lost more money than weight, more self esteem than inches, and more time on the edge of insanity repeatedly doing the same thing expecting different results, I finally realized what I really needed was to drop those weights before the physical weight would follow.

After my divorce I retired from dieting. I was ready to change my entire life from the inside out. I started with vowing to commit to myself the way I had been committed to my husband. In the past when I would deviate from my healthy eating plan I would berate myself with horrible name-calling, and then I would question my desire. I'd say if I wanted it bad enough then I wouldn't deviate, when that wasn't true. Unlike the compassion I had shown my husband when he was unfaithful, I had only wrath for my shortcomings.

That was going to change. It was time I used all the qualities that according to my husband made me a great wife, and direct those for *me* to have a great life. I had an unfailing faith in my husband that the day would come when he would be the husband I had envisioned him to be. That day did come, but I wasn't the wife he would end up being a great husband to. I was at peace with that because the time in my life had come when I had completely surrendered to the idea that the way I thought my life had to go for me to be happy could actually not be the way after all, to the idea that my first marriage was a gift even though it ended, and to the idea that even though I had spent 20 years struggling with weight, my time had come for a breakthrough.

I didn't know how and I had released the idea of when, but I was convinced that the weight would be dropped from the inside out. There would be no point in weighing myself on a scale because the weight I needed to lose the most couldn't be measured on a manmade scale. No the weight that needed to be dropped first was all that the dwarfs had spoken into my life. I had to drop the weight of the lie I had believed that because I was 40 lbs heavier, it meant I wasn't good enough. I had to drop the weight that I didn't deserve to receive a card filled with love instead of meanness. All the animal kingdom Valentine's Day cards carried a weight that

I had picked up that I needed to drop. Just because someone dished out meanness, didn't mean I had to hold on to it and analyze it and cuddle it for years. I could simply drop it, and my time had come to drop it.

Bit by bit, as I addressed these things my physical weight began to decrease. The program I decided to join was Jenny Craig because I needed someone else to take care of the food while I worked on my emotions and spiritual health. Every single day my meals were planned for me, and as long as I ate what was planned, the physical weight was going down. Holding that part of my physical life constant allowed me psychological space to address the other weights.

To this day, that's why I am an advocate for preplanned programs if you are a person who is overwhelmed with life. When it's challenging to pull yourself out of bed, it's nearly impossible to sit down and plan six healthy meals equally spaced throughout the day. A lot of my frustration with people who had the "just do it" attitude about weight loss obviously were people who had not come face-to-face with enough life challenges to show compassion for those of us who struggled to "just do it", especially when getting both feet on the floor in the morning to start the day was a struggle. But the irony of it all is that I had carried that "just do it" mindset myself and had given that advice through the years. But life hadn't yet balanced my views or my perspective or crushed every belief I had when I was spitting that advice out to those struggling.

With the extra weight I added during my pregnancy, I had at least 70 lbs to lose to get to a healthy weight. But as soon as I would approach 205 I would regain 10-15 lbs. That number had a strong association with pain for me. I began my six-month pregnancy at 205 lbs and when it ended I was at 246 lbs. It was the darkest time of my life. It was painful and I had associated all of that pain with weighing 205 lbs, and so when I reached 205, instead of pushing to go below that number, I would push and go above it. The bottom line is that I wanted to get away from all that number stood for in my mind. In my mind it wasn't just 205 lbs. For me, it meant a time when I allowed myself to believe God had answered a prayer I had since I was a child to allow me to have a family of my own. To me 205 lbs meant a time when I jumped without a safety net of considering that anything could go so devastatingly wrong that my entire spirit would be broken. To me 205 lbs meant I was on a path that would lead to tragedy. No, 205 lbs wasn't just a number on the scale. It was a weight that occupied my body, my mind, my emotions, and all of the psychological space needed to move forward in my life. It was as if there was an "occupied" sign on the door of my life that would allow me to move forward and I didn't know how to open it and get rid of all of that weight. Sure, I was supposed to eat the Jenny Craig meals and the physical weight would go down, but the weight of my past pressed on my logic so heavily, I did the illogical and would binge eat every single time I reached 205 lbs.

This went on for four years until I met with a therapist who, after extensive diagnosis, told me that not only had I experienced clinical depression, but I had P.T.S.D. (Post Traumatic Stress Disorder). PTSD is often associated with people returning from war. I could relate to that, because in many ways I was returning from war. I had all the parts of my body, but there were definitely areas of my psyche that had been amputated by the bomb of betrayal. There were parts of my faith that had metal shrapnel lodged so deeply that I was so wounded I didn't have strength to hope. My heart had been pumped with tear gas and it cried for clean oxygen, and yet every beat pushed the poisonous gas of trauma deeper and deeper, creating gallons of poison that left my heart and went to every area of my body with every molecule of blood that flowed. I could easily grasp that what I experienced was similar to what the valiant men and women who serve our country experience as they leave all they know to protect our safety. In some ways I could even identify with leaving my family.

No one could relate to what I was going through. The women in my family who wanted children had them. The women in my family who wanted to stay married had stayed married. The women in my family had leaned on the Lord and HE had delivered them from their pains. But I, on the other hand, had not received deliverance. In fact, it was obvious that I was going to fall in the category of people God made the choice to leave the thorn in the life. Sometimes we're delivered out and sometimes we're delivered with the ability to stay in. I was still in my situation.

After my husband had moved out and the doctors had removed my baby, my emotional self was returning from the war. My ability to hope, my ability to believe I could be happy again, my ability to believe in love had all been amputated in my war. There weren't any prosthetics for hope, love, and belief. Nothing could fill in what I had lost to allow me to operate as if I still had those qualities. Unlike a physical amputation, emotional amputations handicap you in ways seen and unseen.

Now that I had the diagnosis, the question was what to do with it? There isn't any medicine to numb the pain from hope being amputated. There isn't any surgery that can replace a belief system. There aren't any oxygen chambers to purify a heart full of tear gas that continued to pump from deep within.

While this awareness of why I sabotaged my weight loss was great, the solution about what to do about it remained elusive. I did all I knew to do and that was to continue on Jenny Craig to get to 205 lbs and regain back to 218 lbs. It wasn't until I relocated to Atlanta that a possible solution revealed itself.

After my divorce I had gotten on Facebook to try to establish myself socially in a way that would allow me to control when I responded and if I responded at all. My emotional wounds left me sensitive to comments that seemed innocent, but could tear me apart. It was nice to reconnect with friends on my terms and not cringe the way I did in person when the inevitable topic of being married and how many kids I had would always come up. While that question was beginning to sting less and less, it still hurt and I still cried about it. I still carried shame from not being able to get my weight off. I still carried shame from my husband cheating on me. I still carried shame from renewing my marriage vows after discovering the first episode of infidelity, reading hundreds of books, praying without ceasing as I was called to do as a believer, only to find out my husband was still seeing someone else through it all. I had so strongly associated my worth with being intelligent that even that had been uprooted. I felt like a fool. A woman who had been played in one of the oldest games that men and women play by partially loving and partial truth telling. I still carried shame for believing so deeply that love could conquer all. It was as if life was making a fool of my faith and me.

So Facebook was a great way to collect friends at a distance, and yet it felt good for these people to comment on my posts and ask about my day. I would post about my workouts and my weight loss, but then not disclose how it was the same 15 lbs that came back, over and over again. I had lost 41 lbs and that was something worthy of respect and it was apparent in my before and after pictures, but the shame wasn't able to show up in the photos. No the shame couldn't be packaged in a digital image. It was packaged neatly in my entire being.

I ended up meeting some really great people on Facebook who had some depth to their conversation beyond finding a man and having a baby. Most of my friends on Facebook were involved in fitness challenges to drop weight or enter fitness competitions. I loved waking up early in the morning to see what everyone was doing for the day and to log in my activity. Eventually I met a guy who had amazing before and after pictures of dramatic weight loss. After reading his story I found out he was a surgeon and had undergone a weight loss surgery called Lap Band. He was a very close friend to one of my sorority sisters and so we eventually connected and he shared the details of the Lap Band. I instantly thought that would really be nice to have some support to help me with the portion of food I could handle. I was sold on working out almost every day of the week, but I continued to struggle with binge eating, emotional eating, and sabotage. The issue was that I wasn't obese, or so I thought. But I was back north of 205 lbs and according to the BMI charts I was obese.

I contacted my physician back in North Carolina to discuss his opinion of me having bariatric surgery. To my surprise, he was very supportive. In my mind I thought he would tell me to work harder. Shame was so pervasive in all of my thinking that I just assumed that even my doctor would say something about my investigating a new possibility for myself as not being adequate. He had me in tears from the way he talked about how hard I had worked for so many years and how long I had hoped and believed that my husband would reconcile our marriage vows, all to my emotional detriment.

"Cledra, I'm not sure you respect how much you've gone through emotionally. Not everyone makes it, and I don't want you to get to the point of no return emotionally and lose hope permanently. There is no shame in getting help, especially when you've spent four years devoted to getting past this." My tears flowed.

He was right. I was so focused on surviving that I never took the time to really take stock in just what I had survived. Because I was a pharmaceutical sales representative, I knew the data. I knew that 10 people killed themselves every single day in this country. I knew the fragility of sanity and I had witnessed the loss of it many times in my professional career by people who were like me. They looked like they were doing alright, but they carried emotional weight and possibly even shared my diagnosis of PTSD, and the day came when they broke and broke permanently. They started hearing voices, they started hallucinating, they were mentally ill, and for some there was no return. My doctor had brought me to tears, but at the same time he had unknowingly lifted a few pounds of shame.

For the first time, my perspective on my life was that I wasn't inadequate. Perhaps I was broken and in need of help and not beyond repair in ways I had grown to believe. There was hope for me to get below 205 lbs.

The impact of my weight cycling like a yo-yo from 205 to 218 to 205 to 218 for four years had caused me to have uncontrolled hypertension for two of those four years. My hard head combined with my cloud of shame prevented me from taking the necessary medication my doctor had pleaded with me to consider. But the consequences of staying in my fog were beginning to outweigh the fear I had, and I had a glimmer of hope again.

I decided to borrow hope from my doctor. He believed Lap Band surgery would help me and I did still believe in him, and so I went through the necessary medical tests to see if I qualified for Lap Band. It seemed the only problem was that I was only obese and the current guidelines required the patient to be morbidly obese. As fate would have it, in December of that same year the FDA changed the guidelines to approve a patient who was obese, with one additional co-existing disease associated with obesity. It seemed like the combination platter of being hardheaded in a cloud of shame and not taking medicine to relieve my hypertension, was going to be a gift. I had documented medical history of both of the requirements.

I did an emotional exhale. Something seemed to be working for me. A door appeared that I wanted to open. That's the lingering side effect of tragedy. You can mistakenly think that because the last door closed so tragically you conclude all doors are permanently closed. The effects of trauma are insidious and subtle.

In spite of the new door, in some ways I felt like a hypocrite. For so many years I had pointed my finger at people who had weight loss surgery as undisciplined people who lacked focus and resolve. But life hadn't dealt with me in a way to soften me to unseen challenges of weight loss.

Most people who become morbidly obese had their own dwarfs in their past that were much more severe than mine. For example, in one instance, the correlation of molestation and obesity is staggering. That wasn't my story, but like I said, my heart had been crushed to a point where I had compassion for surgical intervention. I knew how hard I could work and yet I couldn't get past 205 lbs, at least not on my own, and 48 months was certainly not a short period of time by any standard to lose the remaining 40 lbs I needed to lose.

Despite the weight of hypocrisy added to my weight of shame and PTSD, I still moved forward to have the surgery. I shielded myself from any comments by going to the hospital alone. Someone from the doctor's office took me to the hospital and then to a hotel afterward to recover. I had to travel several hours to have the surgery because my comfort level with the surgeon I had met on Facebook exceeded my comfort level with finding a new surgeon. He was several hours away, but driving four hours paled in comparison to struggling with my weight for four years.

The surgery was a success in that I obviously survived and I got past 205 lbs. In fact, over 30 lbs below that weight hurdle. It was a tearful journey as the final pounds from all that I had experienced peeled off of my body and my psyche. I worked with not only a therapist, but a coach with the same fervent determination and commitment I had used to try to save my marriage. Pound by pound and workout after workout followed by therapy session after therapy session followed by coaching session after coaching session, the lights of my life started to come back on. It was as if I had been given access to a dimmer switch and I was slowly turning the lights up higher and higher.

My cloud of shame was fading and the tear gas that had occupied my heart was being replaced with tears of joy and hope. I was falling in love. In love with hope. In love with possibility. In love with creating something new out of all that I had been through, and part of that something new is the book you are holding. The journey has been painful to give birth to this book, but it has been incredibly liberating, and it's that very liberation that I want to invite into your life. I'm going to make the assumption that you picked up a book about losing weight because you have weight to lose. It is my sincere heartfelt intention to walk you through dropping all unnecessary weight from your life. So with that being said, let's get into some action steps for you to take to drop your excess body weight.

PlanBE Action Steps to Drop the Weight of Excess Body Weight

IDENTIFY:

1. List all of the programs you have purchased and tried over the last five years.

2. Beside each program write how much weight you lost.

3. Beside each program write how long you stayed committed (truthfully).

4. What are the pros of each of the programs?

DROP IT:

Combine the pros from all of the programs above and make a single list. You have now created what works for you.

If any one of the programs gives you all of the pros, then revisit that program. If not, it's time to drop the weight of denial and own what works and what doesn't work for you.

Take the longest time commitment you have in the above programs and vow to make your next commitment a lifelong commitment.

REPLACE IT:

What has it cost you financially, emotionally, and physically to continue joining and quitting programs?

Write vows to yourself that you will end the cycle of starting and stopping by doing your due diligence of creating a program that works for you (see your list of personal pros).

Make a lifelong commitment to your best health.

Chapter 6:

The Weight of the V.A.L.E.Y.

Validation

Appreciation, Acceptance, Applause

Love

Expectations

Yesterday

After my divorce, I had come to a point where I realized I was the common denominator in all of the relationships I had, and in spite of the way they ended they all included me. I had also been on the couch for almost 20 years in therapy, attended what seemed like almost every support group to save my marriage and my mind through the unraveling of what I thought would be my life, so I was well equipped with analyzing behavior and it was time to just focus on my own. When I looked at all of the men I had been involved with there seemed to be a theme that I call the V.A.L.E.Y. At some point I was looking for Validation, Appreciation, Love, Expectations, and looking at Yesterday.

One of the major side effects of growing up as an obese child is an underlying insecurity that at any point someone is going to slam you for your appearance. This cloud of humiliation was always on standby to rain on what seemed like a great day.

I stopped dating for two years after my divorce to really investigate why I continued to invite emotionally unavailable men with an inability to love with integrity. I was okay with the crumbs they offered because I was so empty on the inside that even a little bit of validation, no matter how unhealthy, caused me to latch on. I had this belief that validation could only come from relationship status because if a guy chose me, in some way that meant that I was special. This belief led me to give all of my power of choice away, time after time. And if I wasn't chosen, it was never because the guy had issues; it was always because I wasn't small enough, pretty enough, or "hip" enough for him.

Most of the men I dated were engineers, soon-to-be attorneys or doctors, or some other profession that carried some kind of stereotypical stamp that meant being exceptional. I didn't have the ability to look past the resume into the heart because my need to be validated caused me to ignore my need to be treated with respect. The roots of this need to be validated externally didn't come from not feeling loved by my parents. In fact, just the opposite. I felt adored and cherished by my parents. My issue was that no one else shared their adoration. It would take many years of emotionally damaging choices for me to learn that the most important person withholding validation from making me feel like I was okay was actually *me*. Mistakenly believing it was an outside job cost me years of self-inflicted pain.

In those two years of not dating, of saying no to every offer to dinner, a movie, or whatever exciting thing may be happening, something amazing happened. I grew to love my own company. Not in a "I don't need a man, I can do everything myself" masquerade kind of way, but from a deep, centered place.

As a Christian woman my worth was determined at Calvary. I was to die for and that fact couldn't be destroyed by anyone else. That fact couldn't be changed by any status change the world could offer. Calvary, where the innocent ONE died for me because of a love greater than any other love possible, permanently stamped priceless on my being and my essence. I had struggled for years with my self-esteem, but in those two years, I decided to lose my self-esteem permanently.

The problem with self esteem is "self". The "self" that tries to separate us into categories defined by this finite world. Mother, wife, sister, daughter, doctor, attorney, single, married, divorced, rich, poor, pretty, ugly, or whatever. All of these were just finite buckets we all scrambled to fit in, and if for some reason we didn't fit, then it was a blow to the "self".

A complete dismissal of self-esteem was the way to go. Independent of what my "self" felt about me on any given day, I was a divine expression of an omnipotent God who, with every breath, returned the breath given to me. I was who God said I was every single day. I was priceless when I got married, when I got divorced, when I mistakenly believed I needed self-esteem, and when I stumbled into a place of losing my self-esteem in order to gain God esteem. The value didn't fluctuate like the stock market. External situations and circumstances were irrelevant. The permanent dismissal of acquiring high self-esteem was a beautiful gift and the first step in releasing the weight of validation. I had eternal validation from my creator and I would have that until my last breath, and even in that moment my value will not go down. It will merely transform.

Another hallmark of a person with a history of obesity is to overcompensate with giving, serving, providing, and meeting the needs of others. It's really a secret contract where the fine print says, "If I do all of this for you, then you will appreciate, applaud, and accept me for the very long list of kind acts of service I do to the point of complete exhaustion and to the neglect of what I need". I don't know a single person with a long history of obesity who doesn't quietly suffer from people-pleasing, to his or her own detriment. It's as if we keep a ledger of worth, and because being obese puts us in the liability column, we feel that people-pleasing is our greatest asset to balance that liability. A common phrase you'll find yourself saying, if this is a weight you carry, is "I can't believe they did that considering all that I have done for them" or "I've been there for them through everything and I ask them this one time to do something for me and they're busy".

This weight comes with the inability to set appropriate boundaries or to respect the boundaries of others. The need for appreciation, applause, and acceptance burns the protective boundaries that will protect, nurture, and support movement to our highest self. So we make a deal with our lower self that in exchange for positive evolution, give me applause, invite me into your circle, and appreciate me for saying yes to your every demand. This causes inauthentic living because what people believe about us and what we are really thinking are never the same. It's beyond the go-along-to-get-along cliché; it's an insidious sneaky belief that says I'll lose myself to be with you because being with myself is just too incredibly painful.

This weight was very common with my friends who had never been married. I would listen to them fantasize about how perfect life would be once they found "the one". The one who would always be there for them no matter what kind of day he may have had at work or what may be going on with him personally. The one who would always cherish them and remember every anniversary, holiday, and birthday with the perfectly chosen Hallmark card and the gift they always wanted. What they imagined was a constant appreciation, applause, and acceptance festival for life. Kind of like the triple-A for the heart. I wanted to tell them, make sure you pack an antidepressant with all the confetti for the triple A festival because you're gonna need it.

My triple A weight loss came when I hired Rhonda Britten, the Fearless Living Coach. In one of her classes she talked about the 1/3, 1/3, 1/3 principle. Rhonda said there will always be 1/3 of the people who love you no matter what; 1/3 who could take or leave you, it doesn't really matter; and then another 1/3 that no matter what you do, they can't stand you. The freedom I felt when she said that sentence was indescribable. I had spent so much of my life trying to convince the wrong 1/3 that I really did have qualities worth appreciating, accepting, and applauding. It was like beating my head up against a wall that, according to Rhonda, was never going to move. Nothing in me challenged her theory because I had enough years of living to have my own proof.

The need to connect and love is a basic need for everyone. But for a person who has buried themselves under the weight of the V.A.L.E.Y., the things we do for love are often things that block the very love we crave.

For me, this craving really stemmed from fear of the day when the two people who loved me the most would pass away and I wouldn't have anyone to fill that spot. Like I said earlier, I may not have agreed with every parenting choice my parents made, but one thing I know with everything in me is that I was and have been loved as much as possible by the people I've been fortunate enough to call Mom and Dad. I was also the one each of them would talk to about the other when things were challenging and when things were wonderful. It was like having a first class ticket to a place where love meant staying, and walking away may have been a thought, but it was never an action.

Because I witnessed such an intense love and commitment, that's the level of commitment I brought to every relationship. I didn't know that depth of commitment was something to gauge by the other person meeting me so I would constantly dive head first. And unlike a pool that comes with a warning about diving in the shallow end, I would repeatedly dive, thinking the water of love had depth, only to end up broken from the realization that once again I had been in the shallows.

I craved a love that would allow me to dive. The kind of love I saw in my parents. The kind of love that was forgiving, even when all the evidence supported just the opposite. The kind of love that gave kindness, even when it received animosity. The kind of love that didn't keep track of anything other than the chance to love another day. My parents had a deep love and I witnessed the deep dive into that love. I wanted that for myself. But the thing I didn't realize is that not everyone wanted that with me.

Some people would trade the beauty of coral reefs to a rubber ducky, all for the sake of staying in the shallow end of love. Never risking it all, never expanding the skill set required to dive deep, never venturing too far from the shore of control. It was a kind of love that was foreign to me: shallow love, with a focus on taking instead of giving, staying guarded instead of letting go, and always traveling with a spare. A spare could be another woman, a hobby, or just complete apathy, but the common theme of a spare was that it divided time in the shallows just enough to guarantee never going into the deep end and never diving. I had a history of falling in love with men who always had a spare.

Looking back now I know that I attracted men who cheated on me because I hadn't learned how to not cheat on me. It took me a long time to fall in love from the inside out. That required doing a deep dive within and having brutal honesty about what I discovered on the deep dive. That's the thing about discovering something in the deep waters of love. Once you receive revelation, it becomes too painful to pretend like you haven't seen it. My eyes had been opened to what I really loved and what I really craved. And just like a scuba diver, the equipment needed, the skill set to go along with mastering the equipment, and the way you breathe is very different than those relaxing in the kiddie pool.

Because I had spent so much time hoping to be chosen, I had neglected to realize that I was in a position to choose. The day I brought that pearl of wisdom to the surface of my life was the day that I learned to cut rubber duckies out of my life right after hello. I finally got the lesson. Just because I was invited to dive in the shallow end didn't mean I had to accept the invitation. And once it was apparent the guy loved his spare and his blow up toys, I took the next step out of the pool. My need to try to convince the shallows the value of the deep end was gone.

With the loss of that need came the gain of a love that was beyond words. I knew what it meant to have peace that passeth all understanding because I didn't have to fear falling in love and being hurt ever again. The rubber ducky man could only hurt me once and then it would be my choice to dive. But I had suffered so much brokenness and paralysis of my emotional range from ignoring the warning signs of the rubber ducky men that there was no chance of repeating that behavior. The weight of loving in the shallows was gone… Forever.

Another silent contract that I had were expectations. I had my entire life mapped out. By X age I would be married, and then by another Y number of years I'd have all my children, and then my house would be paid off by a certain time. So were the expectations of my life timeline. It was like a high school history project where I had projected an entire lifetime of tick marks for when major life events would occur. Unexpected deaths, illness, or accidents of any kind weren't included on my perfectly planned timeline. It was almost as if I had this Santa Claus theory for life. If I was good then that meant good was supposed to come to me.

During my time in Overeaters Anonymous I learned that low expectations meant high serenity and that high expectations were a set up for insanity and resentment. The first thing I thought was *okay, so I'm supposed to just go through life expecting nothing?* I struggled finding the shade of grey in most things, but I gave myself an F for setting appropriate expectations. The incredibly high standards I had for myself bled into every aspect of my life. My ability to discipline myself to accomplish every academic goal I ever had gave me the false belief that getting what I wanted was merely a factor of figuring it all out. There had to be a solution to every problem and with just enough hard work and the right contacts, all problems could be solved.

The impact of this misguided thinking and the danger of the weight of expectations came to life for me in my attempt to become a mom. The first time I got pregnant, Hershey and I told everyone the day the pregnancy stick turned positive. In fact, Hershey took the stick, yes the one I had peed on, to work with him. We were happier than we had ever been in our life. We hadn't been married a year and we had a little one on the way. If life could get a perfect stamp, I would've stamped perfect all over my life at that point. The blood work I had to give looked great. I remember the doctor telling me the numbers were tripling just like they were supposed to for a great pregnancy.

Then it happened. What I expected and what was happening didn't reconcile. I went for my ultrasound and all they could find was an empty sac. The baby never developed. I'll never forget the sheet of paper that said, "scheduled evacuation". I remember thinking *evacuation? How cold. How insensitive. How clinical.* It was such an abrasive term to use for a time that was stamped perfect.

That's the thing about stamps and labels. Once you've attached them to a specific outcome it's very difficult to remove them. It's no different than removing a physical label. There's almost always some scrubbing you have to do to remove all of the adhesive.

It's no different in the spiritual world. Once an attachment has been made, it requires scrubbing to remove it all and it hurts. It hurts to scrub and to be scrubbed.

Because that pregnancy was unexpected and unplanned it was somewhat easy for me to return to a place of "well I wasn't expecting that anyway so it's really not that bad". It was the best I could do at the time with the limited coping skills I had to deal with things not going as planned or expected. I threw myself into what I could control, which for years had been exercising and dieting. I could focus on numbers, workouts, protein, and grams of fat and carbs, all to distract me from the things I couldn't control. That's why I know that programs that only focus on what to put in your body will always fall short.

The impact of things not going as planned kept the weight of yesterday in the forefront of everything. I couldn't dream new dreams because I replayed yesterday at every opportunity. Unlike the other weights, the weight of yesterday can actually be beneficial. Similar to the way that lifting heavy weights in the gym cause muscle development, lifting the weight of yesterday can cause positive development – if we lift it properly. Yesterday's weight is great to lift when it's used to reveal what worked for us, what didn't, and what we need to permanently change considering the years of evidence supporting change. For me this proved to be true in the area of dating.

From my freshman year of college to the day I met my first husband, I had gone from relationship to relationship with no time reflecting on my role in the end of the relationship or a thorough look at how I was dating the same man over and over just in a different body with a different name, with the same outcome. I never lifted the weight of "yesterday's" boyfriends. As a result, I failed to learn lessons that would've elevated the quality of my relationships. I traded reflection and time alone for time hunting.

I remember one relationship ending and needing Kleenex because I was so hurt by the way it ended. As I was buying the Kleenex at a drug store, I met a man. In a couple of days I was hooked up with him and the reason for the Kleenex had faded. I was the classic reflection of the saying, "to get over someone old you get under someone new". This resulted in a series of very unhealthy relationships.

While I don't want to spend this time talking about the role of the individual men I was involved with, I want to highlight that I was the common denominator in every single relationship, and there were themes that I can address from all of the men. They were all very arrogant. I learned when I did stop to lift the weight of yesterday that I was attracted to arrogance because it was what I thought I lacked. Still healing from the side effect of growing up as an obese child, I lacked the confidence to honor my personal truth, and so I was attracted to men who honored their truth, even if it was at the expense of my feelings or best interest.

Another quality they all had is that they were inconsistent. They would do a full court press to get me into the relationship and it was as if they all knew the exact moment when I had genuine feelings, because it was consistently at that time that they would stop calling as often, stop asking me out as much, and stop professing their desire to be with me. It was like a power shift and I would start chasing for attention and begging for time by repeatedly asking what's wrong and why aren't we doing what we used to do. The more I chased the faster they ran and the more I pleaded to do more things together the busier their schedule became with activities that didn't include me.

Once I decided to lift the weight of yesterday I discovered the chase made me feel like I was in some ways redeeming myself from my past life of being obese. I didn't have the strength to walk away once they walked or the awareness of the value of what I brought to the relationship. I devalued my input and focused solely on the outcome of whether they wanted to be with me as the single way to measure my personal value. I hadn't learned to separate my input and another person's reception of that input. I hadn't learned to detach from the outcomes of life because I mistakenly assumed that great input always resulted in great output. I dismissed the human factor of changed minds, inauthentic interactions, and the huge tendency for people to send their representative the first few months of a relationship until the truth is revealed.

Failing to lift the weight of yesterday cost me years of feeling like I was starring in my very own soap opera. Lots of drama and excitement followed by heartbreak was the cycle that I lived throughout my entire decade of my 20s. Always believing that finding the right man instead of working to become the right woman was a way of being came with a very high price. It wasn't until after I was married and divorced at 37 that I decided to stop the cycle and reflect on yesterday and the depth of revelation about my choices and how I was an active participant in having so much drama in my life. That was the turning point in all of my relationships. Again, just like physical weight training over time, what was once heavy becomes light. Over time, when you do choose to lift yesterday, know that in the short term it may seem heavy. But trust that it will soon seem so light.

Now, there is a fine line between lifting the weight of yesterday in order to heal, and lifting the weight of yesterday to the point of hurting. When you reach the point of the weight of yesterday becoming light and easy, that's the sign that it's time to move on. Lifting weight that's too light is ineffective for significant change. The thing that you have to watch for when you lift the weight of yesterday is that you don't allow yourself to fall into regret, shame, or blame. Put it in a capsule of acceptance that you did the best you could with the skills you had at the time and now that you know better you are committed to doing better.

Churning about the time you wasted on yesterday is an additional waste of your valuable time. Allowing sadness to occupy your present life because of yesterday's weight is disrespectful to your journey. Offer your past the gifts of compassion, acceptance, and forgiveness, with a strong commitment to never return – not in action or in prolonged thinking.

PlanBE Action Steps to Drop the Weight of The V.A.L.E.Y.

IDENTIFY:

Look at all of your most important relationships and ask where you are in the V.A.L.E.Y.

Make sure one of those important relationships is the one you have with yourself!

DROP IT:

What would be your ideal shift for your V.A.L.E.Y.?

What would be a V.A.L.E.Y. you could accept knowing you're working toward ideal?

REPLACE IT:

If you were willing to allow your value and worth to come from your creator only, how would that change your life?

If you were willing to forgive everyone who let you down (including yourself), how would that change your life?

If you were to commit to not speaking about things you cannot change from this point forward, what would that free your mind to think about? What would you talk about if you could no longer talk about anything you cannot change?

Chapter 7:
The Weight of Unforgiveness

The bottom line fact was that I was approaching the end of my 30s, and with that came the end of my marriage and the end of my dream that the room I picked out in our dream home would someday be a beautifully decorated nursery. The list seemed long when I allowed my mind to review all the loss that comes along with returning to single status. Unlike breaking up with a boyfriend, the breakup of a marriage simultaneously breaks your belief that you can choose someone you can spend the rest of your life with in bliss without any doubt. After so many years of dating and hoping and wishing to meet "the one", when you think you've found the one and then the one doesn't work out, it's difficult to believe in love the same way. For me, because Hershey had been unfaithful, it changed how I not only saw my marriage, but how I viewed myself as a woman.

As much as my therapist and friends had told me Hershey's infidelity had nothing to do with me, it was hard to stop myself from looking in the mirror and taking an inventory of the woman staring back at me. Was it my extra

50 lbs that took my once curvaceous Coca Cola bottle shape into more like the shape of a three-liter? Was it my mediocre cooking? Was it my tendency to be over the top and obsessive when I made up my mind to go after something? Was it my climb up the corporate ladder? Did I travel too much? Was sex with me not satisfying? Was she prettier? Was she more fun? Did she have a better personality? The list of unanswered questions was long and even if I got the answer to all of them, the reality I was facing is that the one wasn't the one. All of my beliefs were shot down one by one.

Find a man who loves the Lord. I had married a minister. Find a man who has a solid family. I had married a man whose parents were married longer than mine, which was over 40 years. Find a man who adores you, will listen, and is willing to compromise. Hershey adored me and he listened to me, sometimes for hours. He even cut a bad weave out of my hair one morning before going to work. We laughed so hard while he cut what he called a black mop out of my head. I thought I had found someone to accept me for me, and I certainly accepted Hershey. I had checked the boxes and connected the logical dots to what was supposed to create the perfect picture of the one, and I had failed. I felt like I had gotten an F in life as a wife and as my attempt to be a mother.

There had been other men I could've had a baby with through the years and even a few who said we would be great parents. But in hopes to do things in the "right" order, I had used protection at least most of the time, trying to hold out for a family until I was married. And yet I found myself alone in a 5-bedroom house, approaching the end of my 30s and possibly the end of my fertility, and definitely the end of my marriage.

The road after the one isn't the one is full of emotional landmines. Thoughts on any given day about just where you went wrong could flood your mind and literally blow you up for the day. Blow up your plans, blow up your intentions to move forward, blow up your positive attitude that you got briefly from that last self-help book or sermon, and the most tragic, it can blow up your hope. That's the beauty of being in that place of still hoping you'll find the one. You can still believe your formula for success works.

While it was frustrating to date and have it not work out, it never made me feel like there was no reason to hope. But now on the other side of finding out the one isn't the one, everything looked different. The idea of going on a date literally made me nauseous. I used to shop for a cute new outfit, get my hair and nails done, all in anticipation that I could actually meet the one. But now a date meant I could eventually end up in more pain than I ever imagined if I made the wrong choice.

Many times I would call Hershey and remind him of how he had ruined my life. I told him how unfair it was that he would probably go on to remarry and have a child because, unlike me, he didn't have eggs on a timer. It wasn't the division of assets or the visit to the divorce attorney that lingered in my heart; it was the pervasive impact of not only marrying Hershey, but also staying so long to fight for my marriage that impacted my entire life. At least so I thought, and at that time it's what I was consumed with believing. I wasn't ready to look at other possibilities.

That's what the weight of being unforgiving will do to you. With the insistence to hold the other person hostage, you simultaneously hold yourself hostage. Like all hostage situations, it's challenging to have a conversation with the one determined to operate in a hostile environment where the only solution is having the desired outcome, period, no exceptions. People are at high risk of dying in hostage situations and living under the weight of being unforgiving is no different. Hope dies. Positivity is corrupted. Belief systems have a virus. Faith is shot down. Perhaps the most tragic death is that, if left in place, the weight of unforgiveness will infiltrate your future and kill possibility.

I could tell my unforgiveness was toxic because I would get off the phone with Hershey and the tears would flow like a river. I didn't feel any peace by rehashing the past and playing psychic about both our futures. In fact, I oftentimes felt even worse than I did prior to calling him. Over time this became unacceptable to me. I slowly released small amounts of the weight of unforgiveness and started asking myself questions that would keep the weight off.

I discovered that this was heart weight. My heart was weighed down by a belief system that needed a spy ware program to run through and clean all of the toxic cookies out, just like on a computer. This came to me one day while I was angrily typing a letter to Hershey and in the middle of me rehashing the past and predicting the future, a pop up came on my screen that said it was time to update my computer anti-virus software. My acuity for signs from God was at an all time high and I took everything as a sign. Immediately it hit me that I needed to update my thinking about all of this or this would in fact be my entire life story, and that seemed even more tragic to me. If I allowed a sad chapter of my life to then cause me to lead a sad life in its entirety, that would be giving Hershey and all of those mistresses way too much power. I sat down and started thinking in detail about the impact of the weight of unforgiveness on my heart. And not just my heart, the hearts of women I would meet in support groups and online who would share about recovering – or I should say their lack of recovery – from divorce.

There seemed to be three heart destinations where people who find out the one wasn't the one ended up landing. The first heart destination is the person who lands with an empty heart. You recognize them because they've worked hard to not process any pain from their divorce by claiming often to anyone, "I never really loved them anyway; I'm really doing fine". They minimize the impact of the blow they've experienced. In spite of the children, home, and life they built with this person, they make the decision to reduce the journey with their ex to something that didn't really matter. They take an emotionally dismissive approach. I got why they denied how much they loved the person, because to admit that they loved with everything in them would be to admit that they lost everything in them that they gave. It was much easier – at least seemingly – to create the story that the love wasn't that great in the first place and in that way a great love was never lost.

The problem with this heart destination is that they are heavily invested in looking and behaving in a way that reflects a person who isn't struggling in any area as a result of their entire life being changed. This heart destination is so empty that they prey on the only thing that will soothe the pain they ignore, and that's falling in love again as quickly as possible.

I noticed that they tend to attract others with the same heart destination of denial and avoidance. Together these heart destinations create a passionate and heated relationship very quickly, and this fiery passion is mistakenly called love, when in reality it's what I call pick up love. They're simply picking up where the good part of the story stopped in the last relationship. It's not that they're in love with each other. They're in love with the idea that now there will be even less time to focus on what really happened in their last relationship. They're in love with external validation that being with someone means they're wanted. They're in love with the new support group they've created that'll be equally committed to denial and avoidance.

This group of people seemed to be everywhere I turned. They would talk about how their new love was so much better than their ex, and I would patiently wait for time to pass, because on a deep level, now that I had been married, I couldn't believe they really could move on that quickly. That's the other incredibly painful part of divorce. You can't rush your healing and you sometimes don't even know all the places you're hurting until someone touches it with a comment that pierces your emotional armor and sends you spinning with anger and resentment. That's one of the many dangers of falling in love with someone whose heart is in this destination. They speak with a lack of awareness about the reality of their emotional life.

I dated a couple of men who were completely immersed in this heart destination. They started out doing what I call a full court press. I would get these beautiful texts in the morning and all throughout the day, followed by evening calls that just seemed too good to end. That would be followed by a few great dates, until the inevitable moment of tension would come. It could be me asking them more about their ex or asking where they saw themselves long term in a relationship. The empty heart destination never had any intention to do anything other than avoid and deny their pain, so the moment trouble was perceived, they would disappear, doing a Houdini, and poof – all the texts, the phone calls, the appearance that they were so into me would all fade to black. It was because there was never any substance behind the full court press tactic. It was never about me. It was about them using me as a tool to continue being avoidant and in denial.

I finally grew to recognize this heart destination and not become attached to the showering of attention in the beginning. A great way to test if you're dealing with a man or woman with this heart destination is to set a boundary very quickly and observe the response. If they are respectful of your boundary, then chances are they aren't in this empty heart space. But if they come across with the tone that it is their way or no way, then run!

The second heart destination deals with the loss of a significant love, a little more than the first in that they are now victims of their ex's behavior. They acknowledge the pain, but fail to acknowledge any role they may have had in the fall of the marriage. They are heavily invested in the story of being a victim. You can recognize this heart destination by the fact that they focus on all the ex did that was wrong and how if the ex had only changed, then everything would've been all right. Of course the change they're talking about is for the ex to have been their robot and followed orders.

These people have made up their mind that they didn't do anything wrong and that blame is the obvious answer to the reason they're divorced. They take little to no responsibility for the relationship ending. She was crazy or he was abusive. They seldom begin any sentence with "I" when talking about what went wrong in their marriage. You would think they had an arranged marriage from the Helen Keller Institute for the Blind, without any ability to speak, see, or take independent action of any kind.

This heart destination isn't as quick to fall in love again because, after all, "people just don't know how to act" they'll say in their parental voice that even adults their same age should obey. And besides these people not only don't know how to act, they don't listen. What they really mean when they say other people don't know how to act is that they haven't found anyone who will consistently do what they tell them to do without challenge.

This heart destination also uses their ex as a reason to live a mediocre and substandard life. They can't get their life under control because their ex bothers them. They're overweight because of the stress of the ex spouse calling about child support. They fail to see that they constantly use the past to support their present subscription to blaming, being a victim, and having mediocre standards in every area of their life. While dating they're looking for someone to match their low self-esteem that masquerades as confidence. They can only tolerate weak-willed and misguided people looking for direction. Anyone with independent thought or any attempt to challenge them to step up their game is perceived as someone trying to control them. The consequence is that they will be cut off immediately.

That's the other thing about this heart destination. They're so closed, that ending a relationship is often a result of them just fading away without any explanation. They justify this because they're the victim and you're the one to blame. Drama surrounds this heart destination because everyone is always out to get them.

Carefully listen to how this person talks about work. Are people always doing something to him? Are others always aggravating him? Are his coworkers always to blame? Pay close attention also to how he talks about his family. Is his sister off her rocker picking the boyfriend she has? Does he always have advice for what others "should" be doing? If the answer is yes then chances are you're dealing with this heart destination. Know that beneath the surface of the mask of confidence is someone who is the emotional equivalent of a baby wearing a diaper. He dumps anytime without any thought to the consequences, and until he does the work to graduate to big boy pull-ups, he will not be capable of sustaining a long-term, fulfilling relationship with anyone. In fact, this heart destination battles with having a great relationship with himself, let alone others.

The third category I discovered was the entitled Christian snob. You could exchange Christian for Islamic, Jewish, Agnostic, or Numerologist. The part to focus on is what follows, and that's the word snob. This heart destination has a Bible or Koran or mind full of highlighted rigid beliefs that can be recalled without any reluctance to condemn and judge the behavior of other people. This heart destination can be the most deceptive because they have the appearance of living a good life with their almost perfect church attendance, community service projects almost every weekend, and all of the friends that constantly sing "How great thou art" to them for all they've done. If you look closely though, this person comes with a lot of fine print and strings attached to invisible and often silent contracts. Invisible and silent contracts that say, because I did so and so for you then you owe me and I expect you to pay up. These are contracts that say give me my applause for my work. They will deny that they need anything beyond someone to help, but you let someone new join one of their many committees and watch the silent contract of entitlement rise. The fine print says I'm in charge and don't you forget it in every interaction with this heart destination. Because this type of person links external status with internal value it's very important to maintain image.

This heart destination invests heavily in dating using a rulebook. The rules, of course, that they constructed from their well-highlighted Bible and discussed in meetings with people too intimidated to tell them most of it was bullshit. Yes I just said bullshit. I realize I run the risk with this heart destination that they will burn my number and call all of their contacts at this very moment to blackball me from their circle. But, oh well, it's a risk I'm willing to take.

When someone is out of step with the rules, this heart destination is quick to put them into a special prayer closet and conclude that the Lord told them something is wrong. They are very entitled and leave little room for other beliefs. While their spiritual convictions are admirable, their spiritual practices are nauseating. Their gridiron lock on it having to be a certain way makes it nearly impossible to enjoy spending long periods of time with them, unless of course you're okay with never using your brain for creative thoughts or ideas that you'd like to see implemented.

You can recognize this heart destination by asking about their circle of friends. They typically haven't ventured beyond their comfort zone or made new friends in years. They tend to socialize in exclusive groups because exclusivity helps maintain the snob factor without it being challenged. Think country club memberships that were passed down or sororities and fraternities that included having legacy as the primary way for acceptance. They're typically in the VIP section of everything other than when it comes to having a new thought. If you are susceptible to being star struck or taken by status then you may find yourself spending time with this heart destination. Be cautious as they expose you to the finer things in life. Just know they are simultaneously exposing you to silent contracts that will require you adoring, supporting, and applauding them for the rest of your life for this to have a long-term chance.

The last category is the bitter heart that comes with emotions wrapped in a bitter robe. Unlike the other heart destinations, you can quickly identify someone clothed in bitterness. It will rise to the surface of any conversation, at any event, no matter how joyous, and they will be consistently bitter. If you're dating someone like this you will know on the first date by his or her interactions with the waitress at a restaurant. No one can serve them well enough, often enough, or at a standard that is sustainable. They sleep in a bitter robe that they never take the time and effort to clean. They're bold about the stain of bitterness and fail to see anything wrong with it. The expectation is that you take off your rose-colored glasses and get real about life, which in their mind, means not having any positive expectations.

I made the mistake when I first started dating after my divorce of thinking this heart destination could change if they were exposed to the consequences of having such a dark view of life. I spent almost a year with a guy who would repeatedly tell me that marriage was a thing of the past and that people who still believed in it were in the dark ages. He also thought that attending church was exposing yourself to a bunch of hypocrites and a total waste of time.

So what exactly did I think we had in common considering I went to church almost every Sunday, and in spite of it all believed that marriage could be a wonderful institution? Absolutely nothing other than my need back then to feel needed, even if it was with someone who clearly had the single mission of needing me to put on my bitter robe and join him in episode after episode of *As Misery Turns*.

It wasn't until I asked him where the relationship was going and after almost a year of talking daily and going out that he responded by saying I must have misread his actions and tried to make them into something more than what they were because in his mind we would always just be friends. It was an emotional slap, but at the same time a gift because he helped me write the story about the bitter heart destination and even though I know he'll never read this book I want to put heartfelt thanks into the universe for him right now.

So where did that leave me? My engineering mind had summarized the heart destinations I had encountered and none of them fit me. I wasn't ashamed to admit that Hershey was the love of my life. Not only did I love him as my husband, he was my friend and confidante. Nothing in me believed that on that beautiful December morning when we exchanged vows in front of God and 500 people that we ever imagined getting a divorce. I didn't believe that secretly Hershey was thinking as we took communion that in just three short years, *I'm gonna shred her heart to pieces and then repeat until she and I can't take it anymore and we file for divorce.* No, I didn't believe I chose the wrong guy or that we never had a great relationship full of good times. I couldn't deny that he was the love that I thought could stand with me and for me for the rest of my life.

While I was in touch with the pain of my divorce, it wasn't so painful that I couldn't remember the love that touched me when I said yes to marry in the first place. What I believed to be true is that no one really knows what he or she is capable or incapable of processing in a marriage. Who can decide in advance how you'll handle financial pressures? Who can decide in advance how you'll handle feeling disconnected and struggling to figure out how to reconnect? Who can decide how much you will compromise before you become resentful? Who can decide in advance how you'll handle wanting to be alone but still be married? Who can really decide how you'll handle laying eyes on a baby who has passed away? Hershey and I couldn't know any of that about each other in advance, even if we had decided to date longer. Some things are only revealed when you're in front of them. We took the vows to say until death do us part, but I was convinced at best those are vows of faith not supported by any evidence that you'll actually be able to do it. But when you haven't met the one, your only focus is meeting the one and not so much on how you'll stay with the one forever. I think we all on some level dismiss that "forever" part of the equation because forever comes one day at a time.

Because my heart was still with Hershey right after signing the divorce papers, the thought of dating felt like I was cheating on him. We were divorced, but my heart was still connected. It seemed like I was the only one who viewed divorce this way when I'd share how I felt, but I had to be faithful to my heart. My heart destination would have to create a location I hadn't experienced. I enjoyed loving too much to settle for a toxic heart destination, all for the sake of getting back in the game of dating.

Maybe that's why God had allowed me years prior to all of this happening to finish first in my class of Chemical Engineering. Engineering requires a lot of reflective thought and methodical processing. In order for an engineer to create what has never been, a lot of time and thought has to go into defining what is known, what is unknown, and the number of variables. In the absence of that upfront reflective and methodical thinking, innovation would certainly suffer and any new creation would be short lived. Could I do with my heart what I had mastered using the laws of physics, math, and chemistry? I didn't know, but I was certain that I couldn't dismiss my love as something that wasn't real.

I was clear I wasn't a victim. I participated in all phases of my marriage… the beginning, the middle, and yes, even the end. In my mind, even if Hershey's affairs were the ultimate blow, I still had a choice to stay or go. In the end I chose to go so I wasn't anybody's victim. I was also clear that a lifetime wrapped in the bitter black woman's robe wasn't acceptable for me either. The "I don't need a man" parade wasn't a fit and getting on some pedestal and turning myself into a know it all snob wasn't attractive either.

I loved being in love and I loved Hershey with everything in me, and now that I had experienced love on such a deep level, the idea of having a series of shallow, uncommitted relationships was very unappealing. I knew what was possible and settling for less than that just wasn't an option for me.

Unlike all those years as a single woman where I wondered if I had what it takes to get married, I now had proof that I could be committed even in the midst of it not being reciprocated. I had proof that I could forgive infidelity, renew my vows, and actually believe in the possibility of a great marriage after a horrible emotional blow. I had proof that I could have my heart shredded, cry even in my sleep, and still rise. I had a lot of proof to support my new belief in my ability to figure out that there had to be a way to not just survive, but to thrive post divorce or any other disappointment in life.

I started with taking the model of the steps of a wedding and I transferred those to the steps of thriving. I first had to walk down the aisle. I had to be willing to be the only one walking down the center aisle of my new life.

Next was the vow. I needed to make a vow to myself. The one thing I learned about myself in my marriage was that I knew how to commit. I was faithful to Hershey even while we were separated the first time after the first affair. I didn't date or sleep with anyone else. That showed me that when I love I can commit when it's easy and I can commit when it's hard. I was curious what would happen if I brought that same level of commitment to my own life?

My vow was that I would honor the love I had by having a Christian Divorce. I had been a Christian wife so why not continue my Christian values into my divorce? It just didn't make sense to me the way men and women invested so heavily in dragging the person they once vowed to walk through life with until death and then cried the equivalent of "hang them" in court as they garnished excessive amounts of their pay check, created unreasonable demands for child care, and dished out venom and hatred at every turn, but consistently attended church laying it all on the altar. Praising God on Sunday and attacking the one they love the other six days of the week just didn't work for me. The funny thing about mud is that you can't throw it without getting it all over you in the process. I wanted to be clean and so that meant not picking up the mud. I didn't have much company with this choice, especially in church. Selective love just didn't feel right though, so I had to follow my heart and trust that the destination would be one that I could live with for life.

So my commitment to a Christian Divorce became my commitment to not take Hershey to the cleaners in divorce court. That was the term people used about the financial gain that could come from my divorce. Hershey was successful, but so was I, and to me anything I could build from Hershey's money I could build from my own without the permanent attachment to this chapter in my life. I wanted to be clean, so I told my attorney I just wanted to divide all of our assets equally with the exception of the house. Of the five years we had been in the house, we had been separated two of those years, during which time I paid the entire mortgage. So Hershey agreed I should get the house. I remember the day I signed the final divorce papers, I held my hands as the tears started falling. My attorney asked if I was sure I wanted to move forward, and I told her I was certain I wanted to move forward.

My question was what was I moving forward to, where, and how? My body was present, but my mind couldn't put all the pieces together to determine what needed to happen next. I couldn't remember how I got to that place and the most frustrating thing was that I had no idea how to make myself better. There was no short cut solution to moving through pain at this level and depth, and in our microwave society it was becoming even more apparent why the default is a toxic heart destination and not heart liberation. There isn't any medication to sooth the pain of your entire life falling apart. No words can make you feel any better, because you continually hear the repeated rewind of, *just how did I get to this place?*

I would grow to learn that a big part of this process was to get comfortable being physically in one place while emotionally being in another. With my body present in the attorney's office, my left index finger curled around a pen that would finalize the end of my marriage, and my mind rewinding in high speed like a mental search engine attempting to find answers to get me out of pain, I sat in the height of conflict and confusion. How did I get to this point, and more importantly how do I move forward?

Continuing with my analogy of a wedding ceremony, at the end of the wedding, you turn around to face the crowd and the applause begins. It's so important to applaud all of your efforts during the process of thriving after your divorce. In spite of the pain of signing the divorce papers, I needed to begin with thanks. It took all of my energy, but I managed to sit and email Hershey a letter. I needed to shift into gratitude as quickly as possible. I thanked him for the good times. I thanked him for being a part of creating our baby. I thanked him for doing the best he could and I wished him all the best. It was my first step in my vow to have a loving divorce. It was as loving as I could be in that moment and incredibly painful at the same time. Everything in me wanted to resort to the default and curse him out. I wanted to scream, *How could you?* I wanted to hold on to unforgiveness instead of my vow to love. I wanted to rewind and somehow make my baby's heart keep beating. I wanted just one moment in time where the nursery was decorated, where the baby shower actually took place, where my happily ever after happened. I wanted anything other than what I had, and that was painful reality.

Learning to be emotionally tortured but behaviorally committed to my highest good would turn out to be the most challenging part of my new vow. It was becoming more and more obvious why people chose one or all of the other heart destinations. Not being fully present for emotional torture seemed like the obvious choice in the short term, but I didn't want to just patch up my wounds from my divorce. I was determined to truly heal.

This is where the analogy to the wedding becomes a challenge. Couples go on a honeymoon, but I must admit that my next step was more challenging than I ever imagined. Losing physical touch, and not just sexually, but just the basic intimacy I had grown used to from waking up to someone every morning and lying beside him every night. At night I would sleep on the couch because the oversized king bed Hershey and I had shared seemed to swallow me. It was cold and it was lonely, so the back of the couch served as my new way to cuddle without negative consequences. It also helped that I started getting up even earlier to guarantee that I wouldn't be awake for long in the loud silence in my empty house at night. Starting my day at 4 am with intense exercise allowed me to exhaust myself to the point of being able to survive the piercing silence and emptiness of my house at night.

It would be two years before my heart healed to a point where dating other men didn't feel like I was cheating on Hershey. Part of my vow included authentic love. While Hershey had been unfaithful to me in our marriage, a more tragic infidelity is a lack of commitment to my highest self. I had been unfaithful in the past to my intuition. I had been unfaithful to my body by eating excessively and adding unnecessary pounds. I had been unfaithful to my true feelings by dating one guy right after the other and never getting to the root of what I really wanted. I had been unfaithful to my true self, all in exchange for what people said I should want in my life.

This time would be different. I wanted to be a woman who had worked to heal as much as I could and had the capacity to walk away if necessary and not stay only because the fear of being alone trumped a decision for my best interest. I had lived that way before and I just couldn't know all that I had learned from being married and go back to dating the same way.

I remember my first date after two years. I called one of my girlfriends and asked her what I should wear. That's the thing about getting your body and mind back in one place. In some ways it leaves you developmentally compromised. I was like an awkward teenager in a 40-year-old body wondering what to wear the first day of school. Trauma does that to you. It's impossible to move forward with everything in tact after you've been blown apart.

PlanBE Action Steps to Drop the Weight of Unforgiveness

ACTION STEPS:

- Write your wedding vows to your highest self. The version of you that God had in mind when you were allowed to show up on Earth wrapped in the perfectly designed body you currently have on loan. If this seems challenging, pretend it's not a challenge and just write. Allow yourself to move forward, even if you can't figure out how it's going to happen. Don't worry about how, just focus on what.

- Write a letter to the person who has hurt you, but make the letter one of ONLY thanks. It's optional whether you share the letter with them. Make this decision to share or not based on the vow to your highest self.

Be selective about how much you share your journey. This is really about a journey to your highest self and less about needing validation or approval of your choice. If you find yourself checking with people about your decision, gently bring yourself back to your core intent – your best version of you.

Chapter 8:

The Weight of a Suffocating Story

This chapter is for those times when you feel stuck. Maybe you're stuck in a mental rut where you have a bad case of the "blahs" and you just can't seem to motivate yourself to think differently. You could also be stuck in an on-again, off-again cycle with your healthy eating and workout plan and it's frustrating you because this cycle is coming at a price of keeping physical weight on that you so desperately want removed. You could be stuck because you have a family situation that has you anxious because you feel so helpless to change something or someone. Independent of the details, the bottom line is that you're stuck and you need to drop the weight of a story that is suffocating your progress.

I first came to know the impact of the stories we tell ourselves by studying *The Work* by Byron Katie. I highly recommend you Google her work for an additional approach to dropping the weight of your story.

A story is what we tell ourselves to live beneath our potential. It could be something like "everyone over 40 has a slow metabolism, so there's no point in working out so much" or "everyone in my family struggles with addiction, so there's no hope for me" or maybe it's a story you've created about your abilities and how you're incapable of changing. The bottom line is that it is a storyline that you have decided to repeat and rehash internally and to your closest friends to justify not going for your dreams.

The problem is that there's a part of you that isn't completely sold on it and that is the reason you feel frustrated. You'll know it's a legitimate story when you are at peace with the facts of the story, but when we try to make peace with a story that is fiction it causes a resurrection of frustration and sadness on the inside. It makes us feel like we're settling for less than our best, but we just don't know how to move forward. And so we do what's comfortable, and that's to go back to the story.

In some ways your frustration from being stuck is a great sign. It means that you really want out. You just haven't picked up the tools and acquired the skills to move. Being disturbed by mediocrity is a gift. So let me congratulate you... That's the first step: Identify the story.

Once you have identified the story you're telling yourself, the next step is to dissect the story. It's like back in high school Biology and we have to look at things under a microscope to discover there was so much more than what we could initially see. Put the story under the microscope and separate what parts of the story are fabricated and embellished and what parts of the story are absolute facts.

The story I put under the microscope was that not being a mother meant that I wasn't as valuable as a woman. All of the women I loved and respected the most in my life were mothers. Mother's Day is consistently the day women are celebrated. Women who are portrayed on TV or magazines for their accomplishments will often say, in spite of what they have achieved, that being a mother was the most significant day of their life and that they wouldn't trade anything for that role.

My story of not being valued was, in my mind, supported by a lot of facts. I struggled to identify as a woman without the title of mother added to her journey, and so I struggled with myself. Because I didn't value myself, I had behaviors that supported not valuing me. When I started dating I was reluctant to commit, even to men who seemed interested, because I thought *why bother*. We wouldn't be creating a family, so what was the point? But once I put this story under the microscope I was able to reframe it. It was a fact that I wasn't a mother, but my insisting there was a ranking of value that diminished if you weren't a mother was a story. It was a fabricated story, and just because I didn't currently know any women I could identify with who were on my path didn't mean they didn't exist. I had assigned value to motherhood and devalued not being a mother not based on fact, but based on my insufficient skill set to deal with what life had dealt me.

I wasn't able to put the pieces together until one day after work, as if my request for help out of my story was heard by the universe. I was watching my taped show of Oprah and she was doing a segment on the school she had built in Africa. All of these beautiful young girls of every shade of rich chocolate were saying, "Mother Oprah, Mother Oprah, we are so thankful for you." I had found her. I had found a woman who was valued and had never given birth to a baby, and there she was being celebrated by young girls halfway around the world for being the woman, the *mother*, the one to give them an opportunity.

In that moment it was as if God was putting my story under a microscope to show that it wasn't the actual act of giving birth to a child or the title of "Mother" that held the value. It was the contribution that held the value. The contribution that would in some way change the world for the better was what was really being celebrated on Mother's Day.

That meant that I had a chance, but it still didn't fill in the gaps of my skill set. I had an intellectual shift in awareness, but that did nothing for the emotional abyss I felt that could paralyze me without notice and send me to the most elaborate pity party. I needed help, but I didn't even know whom to ask. I already had a therapist and she wasn't helping. In fact, my story resurrected her own pain of not having a child. I had a close relationship with some of the best doctors and access to the best pharmaceuticals. But what medication can be prescribed for an emotional abyss? I wasn't depressed; I was lost. I wasn't anxious; I was confused. I didn't have a mood disorder or any physical pain that could be diagnosed. What I had was a story that, in spite of all of my connections, contacts, and intellectual gifts, debilitated my capacity to find a solution. It was beyond frustrating to feel so stuck inside of my own story.

The next answer to my unspoken frustration came in the form of Byron Katie. I listened to and read everything I could of hers, and when she recommended getting a coach I did just as I had with every suggestion she had given – I took it. What I experienced during this time was that at each level of intellectual awareness that I struggled to gain, a simultaneous assistant from the universe would show up. Just as the episode with Oprah had given rise to my understanding that the value assigned to mothers had to do with the contribution, not the actual birth, the entrance of Byron Katie in my life gave rise to the search for a coach to help me. And just as the thought of needing a coach came to my mind, I sat in front of my computer and the following words came up: "I help people define success for themselves and have the guts to go for it. Get bold. Get courageous. Get Radical and attend the Get Radical Conference with Radical Success Coach Doreen Rainey". I knew with everything in me this was the next dot to connect to unravel the story keeping me in an emotional abyss.

Without a second thought, I signed up for the Get Radical Conference, hoping that this "Get Radical Coach" could deliver on her promise to help me define success for myself and get the guts to go for it. If this worked, this could be the final piece to unraveling the entire story that had been holding me back. I think "dots" show up for all of us, but I think we make the mistake of asking others to confirm the validity of the "dot", and because no one has the grace to see the next step for your life like each of us does for ourselves, we end up getting misguided information when we look outside of ourselves for the next step.

So I flew to DC alone and attended the Get Radical Conference and, true to her promise, the coach *was* radical; so radical that I felt compelled to hire her for the next year of my life to help me. Not only did I hire a coach, I also made a decision to become a coach at that conference and I entered coaching school.

Both steps were steps I could've easily been talked out of doing had I consulted anyone. I can't say that enough. I'm not suggesting that you should ditch your confidantes, but what I am suggesting is that in order to hear the most powerful voice within, the noise on the outside from others has to be silenced. There has to be an increase in being comfortable with waiting in silence for the answer, instead of calling everyone and talking endlessly.

At this point in my story I am new to Atlanta, about to start coaching school, the book you're holding was a vague concept that I would talk about every January, and the pain of the emotional abyss was starting to lift. But to be clear, I was still stuck. I had taken steps to get unstuck, but I had not taken enough steps to be free, and freedom is what I wanted. Freedom to live my best life was what I craved, freedom to pursue my dream of being an author and discovering my unique contribution to the world. And my story that the true value of a woman was found in being a mother still hovered over me.

My first meeting with my coach was incredible in that she cut through a lot of my story right away by asking me to define exactly what I wanted. It sounds simple, but to shift from what you say you want to actually putting it on paper and being challenged to outline the steps to get it was not as simple as it sounds. The fears, the paralysis, the tendency to procrastinate, and the laundry list of random excuses all came to the service. My coach told me I needed to get out of the clouds and come down to the ground to the reality of my current situation and the reality of what it would take to get what I *said* I wanted.

After I completed that assignment, the next step was to meet her in Utah at the Red Mountain Resort for an intense three-day program. The only thing I knew about Utah was that it was the home to the Mormon faith. I had to do everything other than swear on the Bible to my parents that I wasn't going out to Utah to change religions. As much as I wanted to share what I was doing with my parents, it was just another reason not to share too much of my journey, because it will not make sense to others and sometimes it will not even make sense to you. But you have to trust. Trust the voice within to guide you, and don't question the logic because the supernatural seldom follows logic. If you look at people you know who live a life aligned with their purpose, most of them had an incredibly illogical path to get there. Read the journeys of people like Tyler Perry, Oprah Winfrey, or even famous athletes like Michael Jordan or inventors like Alexander Bell. They all had points along the journey to fulfilling their passion and purpose that didn't make sense. Points where everyone questioned their choices and times where it looked like it wasn't going to work. Just another reason to be incredibly protective when you start to unravel your story.

I had no idea what to expect when I landed in Utah, but it looked like a postcard from the Westerns my dad used to watch when I was a kid. As fate would have it, the car service arranged for me came with one of the most personable drivers, who took it upon himself to give me the history of Utah as we drove to the resort. He even went out of his way to show me the massive temple where Mormons worshipped. We finally reached the resort and I was getting anxious to see just what the next three days would bring.

The chatter in my mind was going into overload. Had I

invested all this money unnecessarily? Had I made a bad decision? Would my coach really be able to help me? My mind was like a hamster on a wheel just putting together one unhappy ending after the other and repeating until I had made myself completely on edge and I was so exhausted I fell asleep.

My coach greeted me and five other people with the same enthusiasm I felt in her email several months earlier that made me jump at the idea of "getting radical". Things were going really well until I decided to remove my "this is great" mask and get real about my fears and stop trying to fit in by doing, behaving the way I always had in groups by not exposing the real me. I decided to make the leap and share that while I wanted to move forward, it was very painful. It was painful because there was a time when I believed so strongly in my marriage working and my baby surviving and when it all failed, in some ways I felt like I had failed as a woman. I shared how it was painful to write about losing my baby, and even embarrassing. I fully expected my coach to get emotional just as everyone else had when I shared my story. It seemed like my story was too heavy and too dark for most women to handle. Even my therapist struggled to hold her emotions back when I talked about my baby.

But my coach blew me away with her response. She said, "Cledra, that is a sad story and it will always be a sad story. But you have to decide if it's sad enough to stop your entire life or if it's sad enough for you to show the world how to live PlanBE."

PlanBE Coaching was the name of my private coaching practice that I had outlined on my "dream life" sheet. It was about coaching people through dropping all unnecessary weight – physical, emotional, and spiritual – in order to BE in alignment with their divinely orchestrated purpose. It was about getting clear about our BEing and essence and not getting caught in the traps of the titles of life. That's what I had put on paper, but until that moment I had failed to see how it could happen.

My coach had framed my story in a way that I had never considered. Unlike my therapist, she didn't stop with the sad part of the story. She challenged me to ask just what I was willing to do with the sad story. Unlike others, she didn't sugar coat the gravity of my story with clichés and ineffective comments most make when they don't know what to say. No, my coach had caused me to come face-to-face with the consequences of staying stuck, and that would be to stop my entire life because of my sad story.

For the first time it dawned on me that my story was a sad chapter, but didn't have to mean a sad book. I had a choice to add more chapters. I had a choice to add more characters. I had a choice to redefine and reassign meaning to the events from this sad chapter. In that moment, I realized that it wasn't my story that held me in my emotional abyss. *It was the meaning I had given the story that paralyzed me the most.* And so you are holding my decision to change the story. And now I want to help everyone who will allow me into their story to help them do the same.

So now that you know how I unraveled my story, I want you to identify your story and begin your journey to unraveling. I want to also invite you to be in tune to the universe assisting you in this process. Look for your moments of serendipity, where messages come to you from the least expected sources. Protect your process of unraveling by being selective in your sharing. Be patient in your process as you walk through moments that in the short term may not seem logical. I ask that you simply trust. Trust that you can only do this one way and that is the right way for you. The wrong way doesn't exist. Trust that there are no accidents when it comes to your journey. Trust that understanding how this is all going to work out is not a pre-requisite to it all working out. And when you feel anxious from the inevitable uncertainty that will arise, I ask that you return to this part of the book as much as necessary and remember that this is about trusting, not figuring it all out.

So let's get started.

PlanBE Action Steps to Drop the Weight of a Suffocating Story

There are 8 steps I've identified to shift from a suffocating story to a story that liberates you to live your best life.

Step 1 requires you to identify your story, and I mean identify it in detail the way I walked you through my story. Think about what you say to yourself the most. Think about what you say to your closest friends the most. Think about what you pray about the most. This will most likely lead you to your story. Your story is essentially what you say to yourself about yourself and your life that defends living inferior to your best life.

Step 2 invites you to separate story from fact. In my example, you see how I had attached value to giving birth and dismissed any other option. That's an example of how I expanded the fact that I didn't have a child to a story that it was a reflection of my value as a woman. Do a complete brain dump of all of the details of your story without any consideration initially of what's story and what's fact. In the beginning the most important thing is to just get all of it out of your head and on to paper so you can move forward with it and get off of the mental hamster wheel.

Once you have everything listed and you are well rested, have eaten well, and have some dedicated time for this, take the time to circle the facts. The facts are the absolute truth without any argument.

Using my example from my earlier story, the absolute facts included that I was a woman. I didn't have children. I got a divorce. I needed help. I felt confused. The story was that I would stay confused forever. The story was that no one could handle the darkness of my story. The story was that my story was so sad it would be sad forever. The story was that once something sad happens there is no hope for a happy chapter.

Next, take all of the circled facts and write those on another sheet of paper. Now you have the beginning of your next chapter that begins with facts only. When you are ready, let the page that has the story go. Tear the paper up or tie the paper to a balloon and release it. Do what you need to do to represent the end of the story.

Step 3 addresses our tendency to predict doom and gloom because doom and gloom have become so much a part of our current chapter. For me, I had spent several years either recovering from the news that my husband was having an affair, recovering from news that another pregnancy had ended, recovering financially from being separated, recovering from gaining over 50 lbs, recovering from filing for divorce, recovering from the complete unraveling of my social status as a married woman in a subdivision to a single woman not invited to anything, recovering from the emotional trauma of carrying a dead baby for six months to trying to teach my emotionally wounded self that I could do more than just recover. I could thrive. I could dream again. But my emotional routine was so entrenched in bracing for the next blow that I forgot to predict hopeful possibility.

So step 3 is about making up a future story where you are the star. If we're going to make up a story about your future, which we all do, then why not make it a story where you come out looking golden? There's no evidence other than the past to suggest otherwise, and so step 3 is about breaking the cycle of predicting doom to creating a star cycle, a cycle where you see yourself as the star of your future life story. It has become popular to do this in the form of vision boards or affirmations and I think these are great ways to reinforce predicting your star cycle. In fact I have a free Vision Board teleclass on my site. Go to www.planbecoach.com and enter your name and email to receive that class.

Step 4 continues the star cycle by inviting you to consider who you would be if you dropped your story. If from this point on you never allowed yourself to use the story you identified in Step 1 again in your life, how would life be different? For me, when I decided to truly drop my story, I simultaneously dropped confusion, anxiety, and feeling like I was a victim of my past. It changed my entire emotional well-being to make the decision to permanently drop the story I had been telling myself about my value.

Now the first 4 steps that I shared to unravel your story had to deal with the story itself. The next 4 steps deal with action to take on your part, starting now, to enter your new chapter where your best life begins in this moment. I cannot emphasize enough the importance of self-care during these steps. Be sure to take exceptional care of your physical well-being as we work together to unravel your story. This is intense spiritual work that requires this so that you can be psychologically available.

A quick way to know if you are in a good place to do this work is to remember H.A.L.T. If you are Hungry, Angry, Lonely, or Tired then it's not a good time to work on unraveling your story because your physical state will impact not only your vision, but also your ability to process from your highest and best self.

With that being said, let's move into **Step 5**, which I discovered to be one of the most challenging steps to take to unravel my story. Step 5 is that we're only missing what we refuse to give and so we must give the very thing that we crave for ourselves. In my example I was "missing" being valued as a woman because I didn't have a baby, but when I dropped that story and started adding value to the lives of others and also to my life, I had the thing that I was missing.

Consider what you perceive to be missing in your life as a result of your story. It could be companionship, love, money, a better job, better relationships; the list can be endless. Then look for ways you can give the very thing you perceive to be missing. You may ask, "Well, if a better job is what I'm missing, how can I give a better job to myself when I haven't landed another job?" You immediately get a better job when you choose to show up in your current position as a better employee, looking for ways to contribute to your environment instead of expecting your environment to give you something. You do that by creating the work environment you want to have from an attitude, work ethic, and teamwork perspective. It's like giving yourself a psychological raise. Once you start to vibrate at a different energy level you will attract a different energy level.

Remember we're looking at our lives under a microscope. On an atomic level we are little balls of energy vibrating in response to the environment around us. Applying this fact to my life has been one of the single most powerful changes I've learned to make because once you truly grasp this, you understand just how much control you do have over how you feel in any given situation and that it is impossible to be missing something or someone. What's missing is your unwillingness to shift your own vibration.

Now the next step, like all of the steps, builds on all that we've discussed. **Step 6** is to do an inventory of all of the people in your life. Similar to an inventory in a grocery store where the store clerk is constantly looking to see what stock needs to be moved to the front due to current demands, what needs to be phased out due to low demand, and what items have reached their expiration date. These same questions need to be posed for all of the people you consider to be in your close circle. Who is in high demand, who is no longer in demand, and who requires more energy to keep around than the energy they give when they are around? In other words, their expiration date for being beneficial to your life has arrived.

When doing your people inventory really pay attention to the way you feel when you interact with each person. Remember it's an energy vibration and it doesn't mean anything is wrong with any of the people in your inventory. It's about looking at what energetic combination is created when you mix your energy with theirs.

This moves us into **Step 7** because it's about evicting shame, blame, and being a victim from your life story. We're all wired to crave love, connection, and belonging and so shame shows up when there is a threat of being disconnected. This shows up a lot with weight loss. You have several great weeks of weight loss and then you fall off your plan. But instead of simply moving on, you berate yourself for not being perfect.

I used to skip my Weight Watcher meetings to weigh in if I thought I had gained. I didn't want to admit a binge in the group while others were being celebrated for weight loss. I felt shame for being imperfect and that's the subtle way that shame feeds the cycle of perfectionism, of creating the perception of a flawless image at all cost. The problem with that is that it gets heavy and then we get resentful and start to make it someone else's fault. That's why the second eviction notice is blame. Make a vow to not blame anyone, not even yourself for things not going perfectly. It's about getting to that place of emotional balance where we accept the ebb and flow of life without having emotional meltdowns with every unexpected turn of events.

The last eviction notice is your status as a victim. I'm generally not a fan of cliché's, but one that I do like is that there are no victims, only volunteers. I don't want to minimize the impact of some of the horrific events that can happen, but at the same time I also don't want to minimize the impact of owning your reaction. We always own our reaction and the meaning we assign to any event.

For a long time I felt victimized by my husband's infidelity. I was angry because I didn't used to be insecure when I would see him talking on the phone, but after the first affair, my mind would start doing gymnastic routines every time I saw him text someone and every time he was working out of town. But then I realized that I had a choice. I could work with a therapist and read books about how to recover from infidelity, and I did do that for several years. But then, I made the other choice to divorce and vowed to never allow myself to try to repair broken trust, especially when it has been broken repeatedly. I share often that the only thing worse than hearing your husband tell you he has a mistress, is hearing your husband tell you he has another mistress. I could've spent the rest of my life living like a detective with mounting resentment, but I made a choice for my highest good and ended my marriage, which ended my feeling victimized.

I share this with you to also point out that your choice will come with a price. The choice to live your best life actually comes with a high price because once you get clear, and I mean really clear about what's for your highest good, it will be inherently offensive to people who have grown used to you settling for your lowest self. And when this conflict occurs, you will come face-to-face with the decision to keep a relationship with someone else or to be true to the relationship with your highest self.

It's not always easy. And so that brings me to our **8th and final step** in shifting from a suffocating story, and that is to live your new story daily. Commit to living your new story every single day of your life. It's not about a perfect journey. It's about a consistent commitment that is renewed at the beginning of every new day of life. Make sure the first few minutes of every day are devoted to revisiting what you currently stand for in your life. This isn't just a natural process. It is work to get all aspects of our lives into alignment. It's no different than when a car is out of alignment. Tires have to be rotated, sometimes balanced, and sometimes the air pressure changed. Similar adjustments have to be made in our vehicle of life.

I can't make any guarantees that when you use all eight of these steps your life will instantly become the best ever, but I can say that if you are willing to allow yourself the time to become skilled at working these steps, that you will be amazed at the difference in your life.

Meet Cledra Gross

My name is Cledra Gross and I created PlanBE Coaching after over 20 years of joining, quitting, and rejoining every weight loss program available, including Lap Band surgery, only to discover that while they all worked, they all worked very differently to lose *and* keep the weight off. Where traditional programs focus on what you should eat or drink and how much you should exercise, my focus is on changing what you crave by dropping not only physical weight, but emotional and spiritual weight. When you drop weight in all three of these areas, it doesn't matter what's being served because your appetite will permanently change and you will crave the people *and* the food that can support you, not add more weight to you.

Now a little more about me...

From childhood, I've never been afraid to ask any question of anyone, independent of their status. I've always taken the steps to find a different and more efficient way to accomplish any task. Given that natural curiosity, I found myself graduating #1 from the School of Engineering at North Carolina A&T State University as a Chemical Engineer in the early 90s, with a belief that whatever I wanted I could have IF... I worked hard enough to get it.

It wasn't until I got married that I came face-to-face with the reality that, in spite of hard work, life doesn't always go as planned. I walked down the aisle while close to 500 people witnessed my wedding, but seven short years later I walked into the office of a divorce attorney broken, shattered, and in disbelief that my fairy tale had become, what I thought at the time, a nightmare.

I come from a long line of phenomenal mothers. I was fortunate to know both maternal and paternal grandmothers and my maternal great-grandmother. Mothering was what I knew. But on the day after Mother's Day in 2007, I received news that would change my life forever. The little baby boy that I was supposed to give birth to that December... his heart had stopped. As if that wasn't bad enough, I was told that my life was at risk. I had a very high probability of bleeding to death if they weren't able to remove the remains of my baby. I had to endure another six months of ultrasounds as I watched my baby's body shrink and ultimately dissolve.

Numb from the news, I define this time as when the lights went out in my life. It was dark in the morning and it was even darker at night, because in my dreams my baby would come to visit me in images on a beach and as I would try to swim to him across the ocean he would whisper, "Mommy go back... Go back". There was no comfort, even in my sleep, and while I had been a Christian my entire life, I stopped speaking to God. My faith completely collapsed.

By November of 2007 they were able to safely remove the final remains of my baby, and that Thanksgiving I decided to run in a 5K race. In spite of gaining over 50 lbs, I promised at my baby's memorial service that I would run this race of life for both of us. By this time I was back on speaking terms with God. And then, less than 90 short days later, my husband sat me down to tell me that he had been seeing someone else off and on since we were engaged. I was already broken and shattered, but this blow was crushing.

I define this time in my life as an emotional tsunami. I held on the best I could as I watched everything around me crumble. Already broken from the loss of my baby, I immersed myself in what continues to be the foundation of my life… My belief that the risen Savior has a plan for us all. It was as if my faith had come full circle. I went from giving God my list, to making my single priority about surrendering to God's plan for my life. That's why the foundation of my coaching is my *birth* date and the *birth right* for *all of us*… 8:28 from the book of Romans… "for we *know* (not think) that *all* (not some) things work together for our good for those called according to *His* purpose".

So I thought as long as I was in *His* purpose then it was "all good". I made a promise to God that if the light ever came back to my life I would know that it was a sign from *Him* and I would commit the rest of my life to showing others how to survive an emotional tsunami. My pain was so severe I was convinced that only God could bring brighter days.

And so as you read this, six years after the emotional tsunami in my life began, I can confidently say God turned the light back on, traded my pain for *His* promises, gave me beauty for ashes, and placed my feet and my faith deep in *His* will. I took the ashes of my "supposed to be" life and gave birth to PlanBE Coaching. I live my PlanBE every day, and it is my passion to show you how to do the same.

If life has dealt you a hand that has left you wondering, "how could this be happening?" and you are *tired*, *de*motivated and *frustrated* from carrying *weight* (physical, emotional and spiritual) that you *know* you need to *drop,* then I look forward to BEing your PlanBE Coach in co-creating your amazing transformation! I promise if you do the work, you'll be saying, "I can't believe this is happening to me" again, *but this time with joy!*

Contact me today to get started on the rest of your healthy life. Let me help you build up your strength and confidence. As your PlanBE coach, I will help you get UNstuck and laying aside all weight... physical, emotional, and spiritual. Visit www.PlanBECoach.com for more information.

Proof

Made in the USA
Charleston, SC
23 October 2014